PENNSYLVANIA HERITAGE

DIVERSITY
IN ART,
DANCE,
FOOD,

AND

CUSTOMS

Pennsylvania Heritage
Diversity in Art, Dance, Food, Music, and Customs
Text © 2001 by Georg R. Sheets
Photography © 2001 by Blair Seitz
ISBN 1-879441-82-9

Library of Congress Catalog Card
Number 2001 132060

RB
BOOKS
Harrisburg, PA

Seitz & Seitz, Inc.
1010 North Third Street
Harrisburg, PA 17102

Designed by Klinginsmith & Company

Printed in China

Page 1, Left to Right: *German redware artist, Lester P. Breininger, Jr.; Dalia Yucius in Lithuanian dress; Chinese dolls, Pittsburgh Folk Festival display; Pennsylvania German culinary artist, Betty Groff* **Page 2, Left to Right:** *African American Quilt by Ruth Ward; Native American festival, Sullivan County; Latifah Shabazz at her arts boutique; Greek dancers, Cumberland County; Lithuanian pysanky artist, MichelleKapeluck; African-style dance class*

PENNSYLVANIA HERITAGE

DIVERSITY IN DANCE, FOOD, MUSIC, AND CUSTOMS

BY GEORG R. SHEETS 〰 PHOTOGRAPHY BY BLAIR SEITZ

FOREWORD

Polish enthusiasts enjoy dancing

Nearly 20 years ago, I came to Harrisburg to fill the newly-created job of "Director of State Folklife Programs" in what was then called the Governor's Heritage Affairs Advisory Commission.

It was a somewhat cumbersome job title, and soon enough my role was more simply described as "state folklorist"—a job whose function was to bring public attention to the richness of Pennsylvania's diverse living cultural traditions. My focus included the dozens of culturally distinct groups—based on shared race, ethnicity, or religion—as well as the distinctive regional traditions and even occupational traditions of Pennsylvanians.

I often encountered the comment and question: "That sounds like an interesting job... But what exactly does a state folklorist do?" The job had many facets: documentation, preservation, presentation, public speaking, and guiding and facilitating the interests and aspirations of countless dedicated citizens who themselves wanted to preserve the traditions of their community.

My own efforts in the areas of documentation and preservation took the form of fieldwork to identify and interview community members who had particular knowledge of traditions, customs, and arts. This effort ranged from a single interview to managing a multi-year project employing a cadre of fieldworkers who conducted a Traditional Arts Survey in all 67 Pennsylvania counties. All of the resulting documentation—field notes, photographic images and slides, and audio recordings—were catalogued and deposited into a growing Pennsylvania Folklife Archive.

Such efforts to document the folk traditions of Pennsylvania often produce amazing interviews with truly outstanding artists whose depth of understanding of their cultural traditions is extraordinary. Just as interesting, in an unexpected way, is the fact that folklife documentation often records the very things that people take for granted as commonplace.

So, why is recording the commonplace interesting? What is judged to be "commonplace" is actually a matter of context, and therein lies its distinctiveness. Let me take just one example. Imagine a 20-year-old photograph of a family sitting at a dining room table decorating Easter eggs. Each year in the late winter and early spring in countless homes and churches across Pennsylvania, it is very common to find people of all ages busily preparing decorated eggs for Easter. Nothing unusual so far, except that upon closer inspection, these are Ukrainian decorated eggs done in wax-resist technique, quite distinct from other decorated Easter egg traditions found in Pennsylvania, such as the Pennsylvania German or Lithuanian.

In fact, the designs used by this particular Ukrainian family reflect the designs common to the town and region of the family's origin from three generations ago in Ukraine, and these designs differ from other Ukrainian communities across Pennsylvania due to the historical patterns of which families from which regions of Ukraine settled in which Pennsylvania towns to take jobs in mines and mills.

The photograph may reveal that different family members are using different technology: the older family members are using a stylus that they are heating over a candle, while the younger family members seem to be using a different kind of stylus with an electrical cord attached. Forty years ago, you would not have seen the electric stylus, while 10 years from now, the "old-fashioned" stylus may have disappeared and an even newer technology will be seen alongside the electric stylus. The moment in time captured in the photograph reflects the evolving nature of folk traditions. Innovation may appear in the form, or function, or in the technology used to create an artifact, whether a Ukrainian Easter egg, a Native American beaded belt buckle, Hmong embroidery, or African-American kente cloth.

Examining a photograph such as I describe here is an invitation to explore and reflect on the dynamics of culture, to celebrate the unusual, and to find special meaning in the "commonplace." Any particular image captures an immense wealth of information that invites the curious viewer far beyond the boundaries of the page, into such matters as history, sociology, artistry, and aesthetics. Embedded in the image is the story of immigration and a tale of accommodation and resistance to the powerful forces of assimilation in American life. A collection of such images invites the viewer to reflect on what is unique about the American experience, and such questions as "What does it mean to be an American?" "Who are these people who seem so different than me, and what do I actually have in common with them?" "What is distinctive about my life and my community?" "How can we go about creating communities in Pennsylvania and across the U.S. in which differences are not threatening?"

Fortunately, one does not have to imagine the kind of photographic images that I describe, nor does one need to go to special efforts to seek such images at the American Folklife Center at the Library of Congress or at the Pennsylvania Folklife Archive here in Harrisburg.

Blair Seitz has created a collection of images that capture the history and heritage of Pennsylvania, the legacy of its promise and its struggles, and a taste of its contemporary complexity. The images that you, the reader, now have at your fingertips create a powerful opportunity for reflection and self-exploration, even as you learn and explore cultures that may be unfamiliar to you.

I first met Blair shortly after arriving in Harrisburg 20 years ago, sharing an interest in the cultural diversity of Pennsylvania. I immediately appreciated his extraordinary abilities to create compelling images of Pennsylvania's peoples and landscapes. Blair and I have stayed in touch over these years, and I have always enjoyed our conversations when he would call to seek contacts for particular kinds of ethnic traditions or festivals or performers.

Seeing the images Blair selected for this book brought forth for me vivid memories of people and places I have known. Blair's passionate appreciation for diverse cultures and their artistry has found its full expression in this collection of images. This collection fills a void; combined with the extensive and excellent research of historian and writer Georg Sheets, this volume conveys the cultural complexity of Pennsylvania in words and great images that tell the story.

Shalom Staub
PRESIDENT/CEO
INSTITUTE FOR CULTURAL PARTNERSHIPS
HARRISBURG, PENNSYLVANIA

Welcome sign at PA German Festival, Schuylkill County

ACKNOWLEDGMENTS

Diversity is the theme of this book, and that word also describes the breadth of contributions made to this volume by individuals and groups throughout Pennsylvania.

Some individuals contributed by lending documents, giving of their time for interviews, and referring the author and photographer to others who might be of help. By listing some names here we risk omitting the names of others who were equally important and downplay the role of still others who made the art, dance, food, music, and customs of Pennsylvania come alive before our eyes while this was a work in progress.

Nevertheless, we are pleased to acknowledge here some of those who helped to shape this work into a vibrant and colorful panorama of Pennsylvania folklife. Along the way, numerous people read sections of this book and made helpful comments. Foremost among this group is Ruth Hoover Seitz, who guided the author during every step along the way. To John Hope, the text editor, we offer sincere thanks for smoothing out wrinkles and making suggestions that helped greatly in readability.

Among those who read parts of the manuscript and made helpful observations were Ruthe F. Craley, Eleanor Boggs Shoemaker, P.J. Gryp, Joan Clippinger, Lamar Matthew, Latifah Shabazz, Irvin Kittrell III, and Myron Staroschak.

The writer appreciated help from a strong corps of researchers and advisors, including Carrie Wissler-Thomas, David Morrison, Scott Thomas, June Lloyd, Lila Fourhman-Shaull, Donna and Gerald Shermeyer, Clarence Spohn, Dr. David Bronstein, Mrs. Reba Thomas, Warren W. Wirebach, Corinne and Russell Earnest, Carol Himes, Nancy Amspacher, Ulla Nass, Norah Kienzle, Betty Roberts Salmon, Carol and Bill Schintz, Bernadette Atkins, Frances E. Keller, Judy Weiss, Dr. Shalom Staub, Amy Spillman, Grace Lefever, George G. Lichvarik, Sheldon A. Munn, Ruthann Hubbert-Kemper, Marianne Clay, Deleiby Saez, Lisa Fitch, and Sally Craley.

We hope that readers will agree that among the highlights of this book are the profiles that accompany each chapter. In many cases, these subjects cleared their busy calendars for an entire day and then spent additional time working with the author and photographer in putting down dates, names, and storylines in a readable and accurate fashion. We owe a great debt to Charles L. Blockson, Peter A. Renzetti, Betty Groff, Lester P. Breininger, Joanne Staroschak, Francis G. Brown, and Camille Erice for sharing time, philosophies, and life stories for inclusion in these pages.

In addition, we are most grateful to all the reference librarians, tourism facility staff, festival planners, and parade organizers for the hospitality afforded us during the many months this book was taking shape.

The photography for this book began at the Goshenhoppen Festival in 1982, shortly after Blair and his wife Ruth returned to Pennsylvania from 10 years of journalism work in Africa and Asia. This festival showed them that Pennsylvanians were dynamic in their quest to preserve their cultural heritage. Soon, after observing an Arthur Hall African-American performance in Harrisburg and other heritage events, the idea for this book was born.

In the years that have followed, hundreds of individuals have welcomed and patiently understood the value of the presence of a camera as they posed or performed. Blair thanks them and also his children, Charmaine and Renée, who accompanied him to festivals. Blair also is grateful to Ruth for her invaluable assistance in making arrangements, doing research and writing the captions for the photographs, as well as traveling thousands of miles to enjoy the heritage events with him.

This book is for you who are mentioned here and those of you who made the events and interviews so lively and enjoyable. It is also for those readers whose eyes will light up and minds will be engaged when they come upon a word or photograph they recognize as part of their tradition.

In the customary fashion of passing on traditions, we hope you will pass this book on to those whose lives, work, recreation, and imaginations helped to shape it, and to those who will continue to carry the traditions forward in the future.

Blair Seitz
Georg R. Sheets
Harrisburg, PA

Table of Contents

INTRODUCTION

Pennsylvania has been described in countless ways, but the most accurate description today might be "A Garden of Diversity." If writers and visitors lean to the romantic, or spiritual, it is inevitable that they call it a Garden of Eden. From the beginning, the state offered some of the most fertile soil on the earth plus religious freedom. The combination of these gifts fueled the thoughts and motives of the people who came here from distant lands to establish new homes.

In addition to the material belongings they brought with them, these folk brought their ideas, their values, and their customs.

They packed clothing in their trunks, along with candles, seeds, and roots from favorite plants. They carefully bundled family documents that would help maintain a sense of continuity; in many cases, among the latter objects were prayer books and hymnals.

The early settlers saw Biblical analogies like the Garden of Eden in everyday life. The stories about the Israelites; the great flood; David and Goliath; Jonah and the Whale; and Shadrach, Meshach, and Abednego came to life as they went about their daily chores.

In the New World these stories were expressed on stove plates, blanket chests, storage jugs, birth and marriage certificates, and even on their bed coverings. Plants mentioned in the Bible like the pomegranate, the papyrus, the fig, and the acanthus became icons, along with the maple leaf, the ruffed grouse, and the mountain laurel of the adopted world. Images of angels and serpents were everywhere, and mythical creatures like mermaids also visited the exterior and the interior worlds of Pennsylvania, looking at the viewer from pottery made to hold vinegar and boxes made to hold salt.

Men, women, and children worked hearts, tulips, and "distelfinks" into trivets of iron, bowls of wood, and lamps made of tin. Plates made of local clay showed playful cats and weeping flowers.

A horseshoe placed above a doorway and a rug beater hung upon the wall provided reminders of the garden myth that had as much to do with physical activity as it did with following the Golden Rule: treating others like you would want to be treated, especially those oppressed by tyrants with government or religious power.

Lancaster calls itself "the Garden Spot," and Sullivan County is known for its World's End forest. Numerous writers have noted that Pennsylvania is the only state with "sylvan" in its name, carrying the image of woodlands beyond the era of virgin forests and into the 21st century.

Wood work craftsmanship, Peter Wentz Farmstead, Montgomery County

8

Pennsylvania historian Simon Bronner paints a picture of Pennsylvania that is both shrouded in mystique and grounded in reality. The landscape," he writes, " is wilderness in spots, pastoral in others, scenic and stunning to be sure...." But to bring a jolt of reality to the picture he adds, "It is equally industrial and modern."

Pennsylvania is a place, the historian suggests, where people can commune with nature and appreciate its history and legend. History and legend hold knowledge for use in the future and so in Pennsylvania, practicality, always a key concern, wins out once again. Nature and related folk culture hold invigorating—even spiritual—powers for a modern age, Bronner writes.

Our interest in folk cultures, how they meet and blend in places, and stay unaffected in others, can be satisfied, at least in part, by visiting America's biggest depository of records from the past, the Library of Congress. The American Folklife Center in the Library of Congress houses 1.5 million manuscripts, sound recordings, photographs, films, videos, periodicals, and miscellaneous items reflecting the heritage of the 250 million people who live in the United States, including millions of Pennsylvanians over a span of hundreds of years. The Library of Congress collection, along with countless state and local collections, shows the Pennsylvania tradition has been disseminated to many parts of the globe, wherever Pennsylvanians have roamed.

Pennsylvania's folk culture—its living ethnic diversity—is a rich blend of simple and complex traditions, beliefs, and lifestyles brought here from other lands and mixed thoroughly with the stories and traditions of the people who lived here before the immigrants arrived. Since the beginning, artists, musicians, dancers, and writers have spun stories from those customs and traditions. They have woven threads into a cloth that endures like the tapestries that hang in ancient castles.

One of these bearers of culture, in particular, stands out from the rest, and his work was achieved through word of mouth as well as the printing press.

Pennsylvania landowner, conservationist, publisher, and historian Henry Wharton Shoemaker worked day and night during the first half of the 1900s to interpret Pennsylvania's past for those who would be its future. Giving wide attention to native inhabitants, he also emphasized that many ethnic strains had gone into Pennsylvania's "medley of races."

Shoemaker gave countless talks and printed thousands of accounts describing the things the common folk did and the beliefs they practiced. Shoemaker's quest, sometimes criticized, sometimes praised, was to convince every man, woman, boy, and girl living in Pennsylvania that they should "drink from the pure fount of folklore...." He might also have added that they should put aside the puritanical shame that burdened their neighbors in New England and enjoy the abundant blessings the Creator bestowed upon them.

"If you've ever read a historical marker," Bronner says, "you may be reading his words. Those Lions, Panthers, and Eagles you cheer on the field may have gained much of their association with Pennsylvania because of his efforts."

Shoemaker's residence in Harrisburg was only doors from the Governor's Mansion, and he conferred with politicians, bishops, and people from all walks of life. At various times he was State Archivist, director of the State Museum, and chairman of the State Historical Commission. Using his confidence and knowledge, he became a key member of the state's Geographic Board and State Forest Commission. In the latter positions

Shoemaker was at liberty to name forests, parks, and other features of the landscape, and he engaged in that work with vigor.

He wrote hundreds of articles, pamphlets, and books to solidify his findings, using his own printing presses as well as those belonging to others in his determination to spread the image of Pennsylvania throughout the land. He knew that as Pennsylvanians grew more and more distracted by change in the years ahead, their need to be recognized for their differences—as well as for their sense of belonging—would become more and more important.

Pennsylvania was evolving and becoming more diverse, even as Shoemaker attempted to capture its essence in his writings. His drive to maximize production from the bounty of the land and the exuberance of the people left a powerful impression upon the people inside Pennsylvania and far beyond its borders.

But Shoemaker is only one of hundreds of Pennsylvanians who have labored to tell the Pennsylvania story, and 50 years after his death even Henry W. Shoemaker might be surprised at the increased diversity in the Pennsylvania picture. Immigration in the last 50 years has made Pennsylvania a much richer and more interesting place than Shoemaker or anyone else could have ever imagined 50 or 100 years ago. (The text below gives some interesting statistics from the 1990 census, the latest available as this book went to press.)

The exploration of Pennsylvania's diversity recorded in this book focuses broadly on the traditional expressive activities of many, but not all, ethnic groups from the immigration period to the present. Instead of striving for comprehensiveness, it suggests the range and richness of the groups giving Pennsylvania its beauty and its charm.

To use a southeastern Pennsylvania analogy, we decided to show you the smorgasbord without the need to describe every dish. We hope you will enjoy this journey through Pennsylvania's heritage as it unfolds before you in words and pictures. There is so much to sample and the only question is where to begin.

CENSUS

IN THE 1990 CENSUS, THERE WERE 10,523,180 PENNSYLVANIANS WHO IDENTIFIED THEMSELVES AS WHITE AND 1,087,570 WHO SAID THEY WERE BLACK. THERE WERE 1,160,000 WHO CLAIMED HISPANIC HERITAGE, AND 15,557 AMERICAN INDIANS. THE NUMBER OF PEOPLE WITH HISPANIC HERITAGE EXCEEDED BLACKS FOR THE FIRST TIME IN CENSUS HISTORY. NEARLY 40 DIFFERENT ETHNIC GROUPS WERE IDENTIFIED IN THE CENSUS, RANGING FROM 3,678 PEOPLE WHOSE ANCESTORS CAME FROM THE DOMINICAN REPUBLIC, TO MORE THAN 3.4 MILLION WITH LINES TRACING BACK TO GERMANY.

chapter one

Claimed first by the Swedes and then by the Dutch in the early 17th century, Pennsylvania became an English colony in 1664. For thousands of years before the Europeans ventured here, however, the lands named for British proprietor William Penn were home to Native Americans. They gathered food from the meadows and forests, and used its rivers and streams as trade routes. The splashing waterways also provided food and yielded useful objects to trade, most notably beaver skins, which were of great value to the Europeans.

These first inhabitants saw themselves as temporary custodians of the waterways and the resources on the surrounding land. The idea of owning the land, brought here by European settlers, was curious indeed to the natives who had been hunting, fishing, and gathering

LANDMARKS AND HISTORIC PLACES

The Susquehanna River in York County, a likely Native American settlement site

for many centuries before the Europeans arrived. None of the structures built by the Native Americans survived European settlement of their lands. But some clans left traces of their settlements. Projectile points, shards of pottery, and small items like hair combs and pipes may be found today on and around sites where they lived, hunted, fished, and gathered food. Archaeologists can acquire information by excavating sites of old habitations and recording details like place-ment of posts used in building a Susquehannock long house or what kind of animal bones are found in the pits used to dispose of debris. The kinds of bones found, for instance, might be used as an indicator of diet, and the kind of stone tools might indi-cate trade among other peoples.

Golden Plough Tavern, 1741, half-timber construction, York

Additional evidence of their activity here can be seen on large rocks where they carved symbols like bear tracks, turtles, and thunderbirds. Some of the symbols seem to be geometric in form, and their meanings and purpose are debatable. These petroglyphs, or rock-carvings, can be seen at numerous places in Pennsylvania, including two large rocks near the place where the Conestoga River runs into the Susquehanna, just north of the Chesapeake Bay.

The first Europeans here named the land New Sweden, and its borders took in regions extending from northern Delaware to southeastern Pennsylvania and southwestern New Jersey. They took advantage of the abundant forests in Pennsylvania to build log homes and to provide for life's necessities.

The first settlement in what is now Pennsylvania was named Tinicum, located just northeast of Essington in today's Delaware County. The homes they built here were quite similar to the ones they inhabited in Scandinavia, but some adaptations were necessary to suit the conditions they found in the New World. The most common home was made of logs, and the length of the logs determined the size of the building. Typically, builders used corner timbering techniques, notching the logs with the simplest of tools so they could be joined where they projected at each corner.

Unlike the log cottages of Sweden, though, the settlers here used several kinds of wood and used mortar to fill in where the logs were uneven. This kind of building technique was not known in Britain, Holland, and France, and never in America until the coming of the Swedes.

The Morton Homestead, located at Prospect Park, in what is now Delaware County, is an architectural remnant of this ethnic group from northern Europe. It is one of countless landmarks and historic places that help to tell the story of Pennsylvania's ethnic heritage.

This example, along with a few others, will provide a sampling of how diverse groups laid down the foundation for Pennsylvania and suggest how they continue to build on that base a culture that is rich and distinct from all others.

Coming to New Sweden in 1641, Marten Martensson chose a spot for his home on the banks of Darby Creek and used materials available nearby to build shelter from the heat and cold, the wind and rain. Following the custom, he probably started with a single rectangular room and expanded the house in stages.

On the frontier, this type of log cabin was an ideal building, as it needed no nails and not much more skill with an axe than was needed to clear sites in the forest. Economic reality for the majority of these settlers dictated that their first dwelling in the new country had to be built at minimum cost using local materials. Family and friends provided labor. Forged metal was scarce until rich deposits of iron ore were uncovered, and the people made do with materials at hand. Sometimes they improved their buildings with hardware and window glass acquired later, but nearly everything they needed could be made of wood.

Settlers like Martensson incorporated local stone in the building materials and gradually they were able to take advantage of local clay, making bricks to use in more permanent structures such as churches. Swedish Lutherans settling in what is now South Philadelphia used Flemish bond brick with blackened headers in the construction of *Gloria Dei*, or Old Swedes' Church. They began construction in 1698 and dedicated the church in 1700. Standing at 916 Swanson Street near Delaware Avenue and Christian Street, this is the city's oldest continually operating church, and the congregation retains some of the furnishings from ancestral days of worship.

Swedish culture of all kinds is on display not far away from *Gloria Dei* in another architectural treasure from the early Swedish settlers. The American Swedish Historical Museum, located at 1900 Pattison Street in South Philadelphia, was built on land given by

Gloria Dei,
Philadelphia
Swedish Church
(1698-1700)

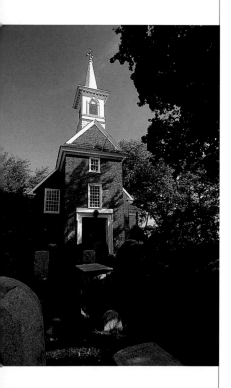

Queen Christina to a Swedish colonist in 1653. The structure is modeled after a 17th century Swedish manor house.

The location of the door, the central hallway, and the symmetrical placement of windows on the façade reflect the Swedish design typical of buildings erected to serve succeeding generations. This kind of building contrasts sharply with the humble log cabins built on the frontier to last through the first few seasons in a new environment.

Evolution in the building standards of early Pennsylvania is also evident in the story of St. Gabriel's Episcopal Church in Douglassville, Berks County. Swedish Lutherans built a log structure there in 1720 and later replaced the original log church with a stone building. By this time the Swedes' hold on Pennsylvania had ended, however.

In 1655 the Dutch coat of arms was hoisted over the Swedish capitol and the new governor, Peter Stuyvesant, promised not to disturb any who would take the oath of allegiance to Holland. Most of the inhabitants accepted these terms, and many lived to see the day when William Penn arrived a quarter century later to take possession in the name of the English government.

With new aims and hopes, Penn established his ownership based on the plain and simple teachings of Quakerism. He was not about to require oaths of the people living on his land since the idea of swearing allegiance to any higher person was contrary to his Quaker beliefs. Quakers in the Old World had been imprisoned for not taking off their hats when dignitaries passed by, a sign of respect and allegiance, and also were punished for not conforming to the official church of the monarchy.

William Penn advertised that persons from all Christian faiths could worship freely in his "Holy Experiment," and this promise compelled religious groups that were being punished because of their spiritual beliefs and lifestyles to risk the long, dangerous voyage across the Atlantic to flee from such oppression. The Quakers, Amish, Mennonites, and French Protestants, called Huguenots, among others, migrated for freedom. The houses of worship that they constructed reflected their religious values. For example, the exteriors and interiors of the meetinghouses were plain, without ornamentation. There was no platform where one or more persons could be placed higher than others in the assembly. All worshipers were welcomed to use benches in the meetinghouse, whereas in the Church of England the church pews were rented by wealthy families and used only by the persons assigned to them.

Built of native stone or local brick, the meetinghouses of the plain peoples expanded as growth in the community occurred. Some early Quaker masons used the Flemish bond brick design used by the earlier Swede builders, but the adjoining graveyards of the Quakers also reflected simple values. Instead of ornately carved tombstones that became customary for other groups, the Quakers marked a burial place with fieldstones or a humble slate tablet. Sometimes the stone slabs or rocks were inscribed with names or initials and sometimes they were left untouched by any mark of identification.

The opportunity to freely express one's faith attracted religious groups of many kinds, including those who lived in tightly knit communal villages. One of the most notable of the communal religious groups in early Pennsylvania was the Seventh Day Baptists. Formed in 1732 by Conrad Beissel, the sect built a community in Lancaster County known as the Ephrata Cloister. Members migrating from Germany used hewn log construction, slicing the trunks of trees with rough saw-like tools common in their homeland. They applied clapboards to the outside to help with insulation.

The Prayer House, or *Saal*, at Ephrata differs somewhat in construction, as the gable-roofed structure of oak was filled with stones and clay before the building was covered with clapboards. Members of the Ephrata Cloister, known for their remarkable paper-making, printing, and publishing activities, spurred a second communal settlement in Franklin County called Snow Hill Cloister. Named for the Snowberger family, this community was composed of widows, widowers, and single persons. It prospered until the Civil War.

Another monastic group, the Harmony Society, built three communities, two of them in Pennsylvania. Founded by George Rapp, the first Pennsylvania community was at Harmony, in Butler County, from 1804 to 1815. The other operated at Old Economy, Beaver County, in what is now Ambridge, from 1824 to 1905. Spiritual life at the Ambridge location northwest of Pittsburgh centered on the Harmony Society Church. Possibly designed by George Rapp's adopted son Frederick, the church was constructed between 1828 and 1831 with bricks made by society members.

Now restored, some of these brick structures were home to successful industries. Others provided simple residences, each for eight adults. Self-sufficiency was a goal for these settlers as it was for many other groups making Pennsylvania their home. Architecture inspired from the European homeland spread westward across Pennsylvania as the colony prospered.

Carpenters Hall, Independence National Historic Park, Philadelphia

In York, Martin Eichelberger used medieval half-timber construction combining hewn wood with the use of mortar common in the Black Forest region of his native Germany to build a tavern for common townspeople and those traveling on the main road from Philadelphia to Fort Duquesne, now Pittsburgh. Some of the timbers are exposed on the exterior as well as the interior, where a large fireplace for cooking and heating also conducts heat for a five-plate stove cut into the wall of the adjoining room.

Restoration workers left some of the *wattle and daub* construction of walls exposed to show how splintered wood and grasses, *wattle*, were mixed with mortar, or *daub*, to create walls between rooms. Eichelberger's next door neighbor, an Englishman, used a modified Georgian design for his stone house, which contrasts sharply with the more primitive looking Golden Plough Tavern that Eichelberger erected. Near the Golden Plough Tavern is a Quaker meetinghouse built of locally made brick by the Quaker contractor William Willis.

The Quaker influence that dominated Pennsylvania after the English took possession declined in the late 1700s. The governors succeeding William

Penn, including his sons, replaced his ideals with practices more acceptable to Great Britain. Many of the provincial leaders that followed William Penn maintained alliances with the Church of England and the British Empire took a strong foothold.

In Philadelphia their home church was the now-famous Christ Church, which resembled Anglican churches in England architecturally inside and outside. The church imported the practice of pews being purchased by and assigned to a particular family. Christ Church was begun in 1727, but work proceeded slowly though the 1730s. The interior design, with the entablature reduced to a square block over each column and the Palladian or Venetian window at the east end, shows that at least part of its design was taken from *A Book of Architecture* by James Gibbs, published in 1728. Some authorities believe the design of Christ Church, the second colonial church in America to have an applied order or formal design (the first was St. Philip's in Charleston, S.C.), came from a member of the powerful Carpenters' Company of Philadelphia.

This Carpenters' Company, America's oldest craft guild, was founded in the 1720s and its members soon dominated the building scene in Philadelphia. Until the 1750s, building in America rarely borrowed from books printed in the Old World. Besides Gibbs' book, *The Architecture of A. Palladio* by Venetian architect Giacomo Leoni influenced buildings on this continent. A signature of the Palladian style was the so-called Palladian window, an arched structure with many panes of glass placed in an important area of the building design.

With its base in earlier settlements, its foundation laid by William Penn and its easy access to the sea, Philadelphia outstripped all other settlements in this region for many years to come. Philadelphia became the capital of Pennsylvania and even with numerous breaks in that stronghold on state government, continued to dominate Pennsylvania politics and culture.

Certainly it is not a coincidence that one of the most revered buildings in American history today is the headquarters of the Philadelphia Carpenters' Company. Now called Carpenters' Hall, this cruciform structure, built in 1773-74, is adorned with four pediments and a central cupola. Robert Smith, of Philadelphia, who added the spire on Christ Church, designed this building and many others that became historic landmarks. The Carpenters' Company lent the use of the hall to the First Continental Congress, which convened there in September 1774 to air grievances against England. The hall today has a small exhibition of Windsor chairs used by the delegates and some early carpentry tools. The cupola on the Carpenters' Company building became an American icon and is much copied today, even on buildings that do not draw on formal colonial design.

Not far from Carpenters' Hall is Independence Hall, a stately marble-trimmed Georgian building originally constructed between 1732 and 1756 as the State House of the Province of Pennsylvania. The centerpiece is the ornate Assembly Room, where delegates from the 13 colonies adopted the Declaration of Independence on July 4, 1776. This building also housed the Pennsylvania Supreme Court chamber, the governor's council chamber, the long room, and the committee room.

Brick buildings adorned with white woodwork and majestic columns became prolific in Philadelphia and outlying settlements. Today, mansions that housed those who shaped our constitutional government are open to the public. In Germantown and in Bucks, Chester, and Montgomery counties are fine examples of Georgian architecture—a wide, central hallway for greeting visitors with the family quarters private behind panel doors.

The extensive wood paneling in Pottsgrove Manor, the Montgomery County home of ironmaker John Potts, reflects the wealth of early entrepreneurs. The finish work in such Quaker homes as the Brinton House and the John Chad House, both in Chadds

Ford, is plainer. Quakers retained simplicity but distinction by building a corner hearth or a winding staircase.

Soon after the first wave of English and Welsh Quakers came to Pennsylvania, the first of three major waves of Germans brought their language and their customs. In this first wave, spanning the years 1683 to 1710, German-speaking people founded the village of Germantown, at what is now the northwestern section of Philadelphia. Here they started the first paper mill in Pennsylvania and began to build gristmills and other small businesses to process the products from increasingly productive farmlands. The second wave of German migration took place between 1710 and 1727, and the third between 1727 and 1775. Most of these immigrants came here from the Palatinate area along the Rhine River. To them the land felt like home and in many ways resembled the rich fertile homeland they had left in Europe.

Because of the considerable geographical diversity of the immigrants and prior movement of people within the Rhineland region, however, the transplanted culture was less than homogeneous.

Coinciding with the waves of German migration, between 1700 and 1775 approximately 200,000 Scotch-Irish, most of them "rigid Presbyterians," came to America, many of them settling in Pennsylvania among the Germans, and others fanning out to lands west and north. In the eastern and central parts of the state, the Scotch-Irish took up homes and shops built by preceding settlers so their influence, at least on architecture, was less noticeable than that of the Scandinavian, English, and German groups. In the western part of the state, there is more evidence of Scotch-Irish architecture.

Some of the most celebrated German buildings in Pennsylvania in the early days, nevertheless, were built not by immigrants from the Palatinate but by pietistic groups like the Seventh Day Baptists settling in Ephrata and the Harmonists settling in present-day Butler County. These and other communal groups had immigrated from Westphalia, Moravia, Bohemia, and Silesia.

By the 1750s there was a sizable number of affluent German-speaking people in Pennsylvania, and they began to build houses of quality sufficient to survive into the 20th century. They were primarily detached buildings set amid rural landholdings, and looked

St. John the Baptist Orthodox Church and Pittsburgh skyline

16

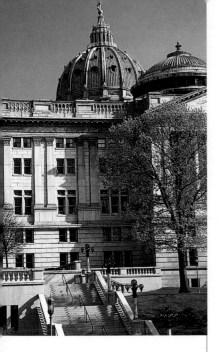

*State
Capitol,
Harrisburg*

more like the single family farmsteads found in some areas of Switzerland, Bavaria, and Lower Saxony than those in the agricultural villages of the Palatinate.

These houses already were somewhat different in form as well as setting from their predecessors, and the new German-American houses were recognizably distinct from those of English-speaking neighbors. Among the surviving houses in Pennsylvania like the Hans Herr House in Lancaster County, these buildings feature direct entry into a rectangular first-floor kitchen with a *stube*, a square entertaining room on the opposite side of a large internal chimney that traditionally was heated by a stove vented into and provided with coals from the cooking fireplace. Builders emphasized hardware featuring decorative silhouettes. The framing of the ceiling was almost always left exposed. Because baking breads and cooking food generated so much heat, summer kitchens were sometimes added to a side of the house or separated, for safety reasons, a few steps from the living quarters of the house.

The cellars in the homes of these people often contained a natural spring, and they were ideal places to store food like potatoes and apples. A crock of sauerkraut might be fermenting here, too, and beverages like cherry bounce could be nurtured along to good use.

The roofs of these houses were sometimes covered with flat shingle-like tiles with the attic space used for storing grain and curing meat. As the farmstead grew, a smokehouse, chicken house, and other buildings might be added. Of course, the most important building on these farms often was the barn, and the German bank barn, built against a hillside to allow entrance from two levels, became a dominating feature of the landscape in southeastern Pennsylvania.

As the 18th century dawned on the Pennsylvania horizon, dramatic changes took place reflecting powerful acculturative pressures. Essential aspects of the old forms and structures were retained but combined in ways that emphasized exterior symmetry.

During the early days of the 19th century, when a homogeneous American form overwhelmed recognizable German forms, the decoration of interiors and furnishings was carried to a level of richness and flamboyance previously unknown. Decorative, non-functional woodwork was a reflection of a widespread stylistic trend, but more importantly expressed the presence of an aesthetic or sense of taste that was not shared by everyone in the province or the nation. These tastes usually originated in the homes and salons of wealthy Europeans who wanted to transplant their educational and cultural values as well as their vineyards, orchards, and formal gardens, like John Bartram's garden, a 45-acre landmark overlooking the Schuylkill River in what is now West Philadelphia.

For most people, however, there seemed to be a dichotomy between exterior conformity and interior expressiveness. Many people immigrating to Pennsylvania adopted the outward building designs of existing culture and expressed the culture instilled within them on the interiors.

When the early German-speaking immigrants faced great pressure to conform, for example, they responded with an intense, mostly personal expression of affection for old cultural distinctions. This practice can be seen over and over again in other Pennsylvania ethnic groups that retain Old World traditions as they face New World realities.

For example, inside the house and the workshop the German-speaking people used the Pennsylvania Dutch (Pennsylvania German) dialect and decorated their furnishings with designs of ethnic origin like the distelfink, the angel, and the tulip. Many of the Scotch-Irish expressed their culture and their creativity inside the home in furnishings, pictures, and household goods. These houses, as the houses of ethnic people today, became miniature museums of Old World culture.

As later migrants from nations not before represented in Pennsylvania arrived here, their influence on architecture was felt mainly in their houses of worship. The skylines of many Pennsylvania towns and cities attest to waves of migration to Pennsylvania decades after the Revolutionary War. A distant view of Mt. Carmel, in Northumberland County, for instance, shows Greek, Russian, and Roman Catholic church spires.

The "onion domes" of the Russian churches are the most obvious architectural features transplanted to Pennsylvania by groups leaving Eastern Europe. Many houses of worship built after the Revolutionary War, even if they do not reflect the owners' culture outwardly, contain interior furnishings and decorations that speak of cultural distinctions and religious expression not seen in Pennsylvania until later years in the state's development.

Architecture and landscapes have not always been the most visible expressions of ethnicity, and even large urban groups built little that was distinctively from their culture—with few exceptions, like Chinatown and the Italian Market in Philadelphia, and the Shadyside and Squirrel Hill sections of Pittsburgh. In the Oakland section of Pittsburgh, the University of Pittsburgh's Cathedral of Learning contains 26 rooms, each designed to represent the culture and history of a different country.

The expression of tradition and pride in architecture and the furnishing of buildings remains one of the most interesting aspects of Pennsylvania's diverse ethnic culture. From the Japanese Pagoda in Reading to the Old Jailhouse Museum in Jim Thorpe to the Scottish Rite facility in Williamsport, ethnic and cultural values are shown outside and inside buildings made to endure.

Tradition and cultural pride in architecture and furnishings come together in splendid expressions in almost every Pennsylvania city and town. One of the most notable examples of architecture expressing cultural values of Pennsylvania is, naturally enough, the Capitol building at Harrisburg. The state legislature voted to move the capital to Harrisburg partly because it was a more central location than Philadelphia, which had served on and off as center of government since the days of William Penn. When the first

Capitol in Harrisburg, designed by Stephen Hills, burned in 1897, legislators awarded a contract to architect Henry Ives Cobb to design a replacement. Cobb presented a plan for an ornate, elaborate Capitol, but funding fell short and a brick structure without adornment resulted. In 1901, a young architect from Philadelphia won a competition for the expansion and fulfillment of the existing structure. Joseph Miller Huston presented a grand vision for a "Palace of Art" that would stand as a monument to Pennsylvania government and reflect the elevated status of culture among Pennsylvania's diverse peoples. Huston modeled a dome for the new Capitol to resemble the dome designed by Michelangelo for St. Peter's Basilica in Rome. Inside the main rotunda he incorporated many elements seen in Charles Garnier's Paris Opera House: a grand marble staircase, a caryatid doorway flanked by two light standards, and a triple arcaded gallery. His plan included an exquisite program to decorate and furnish the building with art that glorified Pennsylvania's democratic government and celebrated achievements in labor, industry, and history. To support his vision centered around a classical beaux arts style and grounding elements, he recruited some of the finest artists and craftsmen in the world, many of them with roots in Pennsylvania: Violet Oakley, George Grey Barnard, and Henry Chapman Mercer. His plan used mostly white Vermont marble in the spectacular rotunda, but he imported more durable Italian marble for the steps. An army of laborers including stone masons, tile makers, glass workers, and carpenters, many from ethnic communities outside Harrisburg, carried out the plan, and five years later the Pennsylvania Capitol was dedicated by Theodore Roosevelt on October 4, 1906. As the President surveyed the building he declared, "This is the handsomest state capitol I ever saw."

Ethnic workers from many countries and cultures contributed to the Capitol that still is admired today, and they continue to take a role in preserving and conserving it under the aegis of the Capitol Preservation Committee, formed in 1982. Many of these workers have deep roots in Pennsylvania soil, while others are experiencing the acculturation faced by all people who leave their motherland in hopes of finding a better lifestyle abroad.

More than 300 years after William Penn laid the foundation for a government that would serve the people and not oppress them, the ethnic groups of Pennsylvania are expressing their ethnicity through their labor, their skills, their arts, music, dance, foods, languages, and customs. Some of these groups express ethnic traditions in public affairs like festivals and parades. Others express their culture mostly in the home, where they may set up small altars and display artwork, crafts, and furnishings from the Old Country. Some families express ethnic culture in door or window decorations and by setting up small shrines in backyards or along roadsides. Some burn candles and incense, drink special beverages, or eat special foods. And nearly every family is touched in some way by the traditions originating from ancestors, whether Native American or immigrants from Australia or Zaire. The examples are almost endless.

After the Korean and Vietnam wars, immigrants from Asia arrived in Pennsylvania and many found work in restaurants offering foods familiar in their homelands. In many cases the decoration and furnishing of restaurants became an expression of cultural identity.

East Indians arriving here after World War II often went into the hospitality trades and their restaurants, motels, and shops also reflect the age-old customs of people engaged in keeping traditions alive. Perhaps the business establishments and shops opened by these newcomers will be the landmarks and historic places of tomorrow.

Those early groups that peopled Pennsylvania continue to influence almost every aspect of the state today, but at the same time newcomers add to an ever-expanding kaleidoscope of cultural diversity enriching Pennsylvania and making it one of the most colorful and diverse states in the nation.

Top: *The Hans Herr House, built of fieldstone in Lancaster County in 1711, is the oldest example of German medieval architecture in America.* **Above:** *Artifacts of Pennsylvania's early Native American residents include beads, arrowheads, and sharpened stones used as tools as displayed at Fort Augusta, Sunbury.* **Right:** *Dependence on wood by Swedes and Finns, Pennsylvania's first European settlers, is noticeable in the structure and furnishings of the restored Morton Homestead in Delaware County.*

Above: *The Morgan Log House is the 300-year-old aristocratic home of a Welsh family located in Montgomery County.* **Right:** *The Brinton 1704 House in Dilworthtown, Chester County, depicts the refinement of Quaker English settlers who were drawn to Pennsylvania by William Penn's vision. Such luxury items as forks and chairs were on the house inventory kept by William Brinton, who built the house. With thick fieldstone walls and an interior beehive oven, the basement kitchen was the warmest room in the house during winter.*

FRANCIS G. BROWN

Francis G. Brown found his life ministry without leaving the home where he was born in 1917. He lives there today with his wife of more than 50 years, and spends most of his free time a few miles away, preserving the Old Caln Quaker meetinghouse overlooking the Great Valley of Chester County. The Religious Society of Friends, including some of Brown's ancestors, built the meetinghouse here in 1726 and then doubled its size in 1801. Massive stones give the building the look of durability, and the unpainted woodwork and furnishings inside offer a view into 18th century Pennsylvania life that is rare indeed. The meetinghouse is located on Pa. Rte. 340, better known in earlier times as the King's Highway, the main road leading from Philadelphia to Lancaster.

Long before Brown's birth, his family joined Downingtown Friends Meeting, and he remembers fondly his childhood days in a Quaker community. Now he has found a mission that fits him like a hand-made shirt.

A graduate of Haverford College, Brown went to work for Philadelphia Yearly Meeting, a headquarters administrative and service office for the Society of Friends in 1958. From 1964 to 1980 he served as general secretary (the chief executive) of the Yearly Meeting, responsible for Quaker business in Pennsylvania westward to State College and including Delaware, Maryland, and a portion of New Jersey. In the course of his work he became acquainted with more than 100 Quaker meetings. He tells the history of the Old Caln meetinghouse like he recites stories of the family and the farm where he grew up. A descendant of the Quakers arriving in this region in the early 1700s, Brown is working to bring Old Caln back to use as a community center after a century of benign neglect.

Brown tells the story of Quakers with respect and enthusiasm. In their native England, government and church officials severely persecuted the members of the Religious Society of Friends, which was founded about 1650. Sometimes Quakers were imprisoned for nothing more than holding their meetings for worship openly. The law, in that time and place, limited worship to meetings within the Established Church.

Worship was central in the lives of the early Quakers, and as thousands of their brethren were being persecuted because of religious beliefs, William Penn, a member of

Francis and Enid Brown stand in Old Caln Meetinghouse built in 1726 in Chester County by English Quakers

their community of worship, invited them to take part in his "Holy Experiment." Many Quakers throughout the British Isles packed up their belongings and boarded ships bound for Penn's new colony, where religious freedom was assured and encouraged. Soon after establishing settlements in Pennsylvania, these Quakers built structures where, according to their practice, they could "meet with one another and with God."

A Quaker meeting for worship is usually silent, as members "wait on the Lord." Anyone who feels spiritually led is free to share insights or "leadings," as he or she reflects on the idea central to the concept of Quakerism—an Inner Light present within every person. Quakers built their meetinghouses in the simplest way possible. They used clear windows and installed plain wooden benches. Sliding wood panels divided sections of the meetinghouses. During business meetings, members used these dividers to separate males from females.

Men and women were equal, nevertheless. Women made their voices heard through notes summarizing their views that were delivered to the men's gathering in the adjoining room. There was no need in these structures for an altar, a musical instrument, or even offering plates. There was no liturgy, no presiding minister, and no fixed order of service. Builders designed these houses with a minimum of distractions that would interfere with each individual's inward spiritual search. An important Quaker testimony is that any kind of fighting is wrong, and except for a small group in Philadelphia known as "Free Quakers", became conscientious objectors when government forces call them to the battleground. Brown was a conscientious objector, and when World War II broke out he took an assignment for "detached service." The government assigned Brown to duty in community service. While he was on another assignment in Connecticut, Brown decided to accompany friends to a square dance one night and he remembers that dance as the place where he met Enid Swartzendruber, now his wife of more than 50 years.

After the war, Brown returned to his family's farm and then took the job with the Society of Friends. "After I retired in 1980," Brown says, " I found my personal ministry. I came to this old meetinghouse and saw the authenticity that still exists after all these years. My ministry is to bring this old building back into Quakerism and to lead it back into use as a community center for Quakers and non-Quakers."

Brown recruited students from Downingtown High School to help him repair the walls of the building and to clear the woodlot that threatened to take over the adjoining graveyard. He helped with arrangements for the Old Caln Historical Society to assist in the maintenance of the building and that Society now uses the West Room as its headquarters and museum.

Workers have renovated a shed next to the meetinghouse that now serves as an office for a regional Quaker Youth Coordinator. The presence of a full-time employee on the grounds assures that the Old Caln meetinghouse is in active, year-round service and that there is someone on the grounds to greet visitors who stop by to take in a part of the region's past still in service today.

Meetings of the historical society and special events like Christmas candlelight services also help to fulfill Brown's dream of returning Old Caln to its original use as a center for spiritual and community service. A Quaker meeting for worship is held once a month, and Brown reports a growing number of participants are assuring a bright future for a meetinghouse planted firmly in the past.

THE ESTABLISHMENT OF CIVILIZATION
IN THE DELAWARE VALLEY
THE COMING OF THE SWEDES IN MARCH 1638

Left: *Since 1926, events and exhibits at the American Swedish Historical Museum in South Philadelphia have interpreted Swedish heritage. A stylized mural in the museum's entrance hall shows Peter Minuit meeting the Lenape Indians when his two ships arrived in 1638 and the New Sweden Colony sprang up along the Delaware River.* **Above:** *In the 1730s a German-born mystic, Conrad Beissel, founded a religious community at the Ephrata Cloister near Lancaster. He and his followers worshiped in this hall on simple wooden benches without religious icons.* **Next pages:** *After arriving from Russia to work in Schuylkill County's mines, immigrant families founded the Holy Trinity Orthodox Church (Russian) in McAdoo in 1901. The church was built with money given by Russian czars, who also donated the cross and a plated icon. The oak icon screen was crafted more recently by Pennsylvania artisans.*

Above Left: *The bell tower of the Central Moravian Church rises above Bethlehem, where Moravians settled in the 1700s.* **Below Left:** *Jews from various areas of Europe brought to Pennsylvania synagogues such ancient Hebrew traditions as blowing a shofar, or ram's horn trumpet, at high religious observances.* **Above:** *Mother Bethel A.M.E. Church on 6th Street in Philadelphia was the first African Methodist Episcopal church established and owned by African-Americans. Richard Allen founded the church in 1787 as a place of worship for all people.*

chapter two

Ethnic groups from dozens of nations have contributed abundantly to the arts of Pennsylvania, and their influence spills over into the American mainstream in many ways both apparent and hidden. Some elements of the arts in Pennsylvania remain distinctively ethnic, while others have become almost indistinguishable within the total tapestry, enriching the cultural "stew" or the ethnic "tossed salad."

In various ways the arts are woven into every major life event. Even before birth, mothers sing lullabies in their native language, and babies are exposed to the arts in the home and the house of worship soon after their birth. Initiation of infants into their religious

ART, DANCE, AND MUSIC

heritage, the marriage ceremony, and coming of age ceremonies like the bar mitzvah and the bat mitzvah are all events in which the visual and performing arts express ethnic, religious, and cultural values.

The overlapping of the arts, especially of music, dance, and visual design, is as evident in these ceremonies as it is in religious and secular festivals, parades, and public performances with strong ethnic identity. Two examples of the joining together of various art forms easily found in Pennsylvania are flamenco and opera.

There is perhaps no better example of the blend of art, dance, and music in Pennsylvania's ethnic diversity than in a performance of flamenco by one of the state's many Spanish-speaking groups. Flamenco, the traditional song and dance of the *gitanos*, or Gypsies, of Andalucia in southern Spain, entered polite society in the early 19th century as café entertainment.

Flamenco dancing by Danzante, Harrisburg

Ethnic dance stage at the Lancaster folk arts festival

Cante (song) is the core of flamenco and like *baile* (dance) it has three forms: *grande* or *hondo* (grand or deep), intense, profound songs, tragic in tone and imbued with *duende*, the transformation of the musician by the depth of the emotion; *intermedio* (intermediate), moderately serious, the music is sometimes Oriental–sounding; and *pequeño* (small) light songs of exuberance, love, and nature.

Both the text and melody of these songs, like the flamenco dance, are improvised within traditional structures such as characteristic rhythms and chords. *Zapateado*, intricate toe and heel-clicking steps, characterizes the men's dance, while the traditional women's dance is based more on grace of body and hand movement.

Song and dance in flamenco performance may be accompanied by *jaleo*, rhythmic finger-snapping, hand clapping, and shouting. In the 19th century, guitar accompaniment became common for many genres, and guitar solos also developed. The costumes worn in flamenco presentations feature colorful full-skirted dresses for ladies and dark high-waisted pants secured with a sash for men. The men wear ruffled shirts, and both men and women wear a custom-made shoe with a slightly elevated heel. The design and execution of costumes is important in this art form as in many other activities that express ethnic ideals. In the 20th century, commercial pressure distorted much of the traditional flamenco dance, but a modern-day performance, enhanced with lighting and setting, provides a memorable, uplifting experience.

Many of these elements are captured in the paintings of Virgil Sova, a contemporary Pennsylvania painter born in Greensburg, Westmoreland County. Sova, whose ancestors emigrated from Czechoslovakia, studied at Carnegie-Mellon University and the Art Institute of Pittsburgh, and eventually earned the title of master pastelist awarded by the Pastel Society of America. In extended trips to Europe, he studied the culture of the Old World and then purchased a second home in Andalucia, a mountainous region of ancient hill towns descending to the Mediterranean with sun-drenched vistas of sea and sky and endless miles of olive groves. The artist's Pennsylvania home in New Holland, Lancaster County, is a gathering place for adherents of old European values, and his exhibitions often feature flamenco performances against backdrops of Andalucian imagery.

Dance, music, and the visual arts blend on another scale when any of the many opera companies in Pennsylvania stage a production given birth by Old World culture. In opera, as in flamenco, the ancient form of "stagecraft" or "theater" takes in many elements of the arts.

An important factor in operatic productions is the set, where Old World architecture, illustration, painting, and sculpting take center stage. Artisans from many disciplines contribute to the performance, including garment-makers, hat-makers, cobblers, carpenters, weavers, hairstylists, make-up artists, carriage makers, and even purveyors of food and beverage products. Another contemporary Pennsylvania artist, Othmar Carli, combines elements of art history, sculpting, painting, stagecraft, and science he learned as an apprentice in his native Austria, to support artistic performances in the state. His work has taken him from his original Pennsylvania studio in Adams County to opera houses, courthouses, churches, synagogues, temples, and other public buildings across the state where he works as a preservationist of sites with strong ethnic ties. He maintains ties with his homeland by exhibiting his innovative work there, and he passes on Old World skills and insights to younger generations through workshops and on-the-job training.

Opera is strongly associated with Italy, Germany, and Austria, but this art form is staged in dozens of languages directly associated with the ethnic traditions of Pennsylvania. Dominick Argento, for example, draws on his family ties to Sicily, as well as other sources, for inspiration in composing modern operas praised for their brilliance. Winner of a Pulitzer Prize, Argento was born in York in 1927. He titled his first opera, completed in 1954, *Sicilian Lime*, but he is perhaps best known for his one-act *Postcard from Morocco*.

Travel to Old World countries almost always reinforces or revives expressions of ethnic art, music, and dance. One example of this occurrence lies in the revival of the San Rocco Festival held in Aliquippa, Beaver County, each August. When this decades-old tradition seemed about to end its course in Pennsylvania, residents of Aliquippa made a trip to Patricia, Italy, home of their ancestors. They returned to Pennsylvania with a renewed enthusiasm for the art, dance, music, and literature of their motherland and injected new vigor into succeeding San Rocco Festivals in Beaver County.

The effect of travels back and forth to the land of origin is also evident in the folklife of many Puerto Ricans who have migrated to Pennsylvania. Observers of cultural patterns have pointed out that frequent trips to Puerto Rico by Puerto Rican residents of Pennsylvania have helped to keep the Spanish language strong. The same is true for those Spanish-speaking peoples from Central America and Mexico. Assimilation into the mainstream English-speaking population, expected by some social workers decades ago, has not happened. Contrary to this expectation, periodic re-immersion into the art, dance, and music of the homeland has reinforced ethnic pride and customs.

Movement to Pennsylvania from regions within the contiguous United States—the American South, the American West, and New England—continues to affect Pennsylvania's culture, too. The number of Pennsylvania radio stations that have adopted a country and western music format is one indicator of how Pennsylvania's cultural life is influenced from within the United States as well as regions from around the globe. Radio and television stations with Spanish programming show the effect, too, just as media that carry "New Orleans-style jazz," "Motown," and bluegrass music give further credence to cross-cultural experience within the United States. On the other hand, salsa, calypso, zydeco, reggae, and many other music types have infiltrated Pennsylvania music from places farther away. With these music forms of relatively recent vintage in Pennsylvania stand the age-old minuets, waltzes, polkas, and jigs of earlier days.

Dancing often is a special reflection of ethnic life in a community. Not only is it a physical activity, it also expresses social interaction between individuals and a group. The music, costumes, and background join with the dancers' movements and patterns to give a glimpse of a culture and its heritage. Although the steps in ethnic dances often are the same, differences in speed, costuming, and performance make the dances different from each other.

Many of what today are known as folk dances—ethnic dances that have gone through changes over time—have spread throughout the American folk scene just as the immigrants who brought them here have spread throughout Pennsylvania and the nation. Many of the dances were performed in close-knit communities in time-honored fashion at weddings, christenings, and on important holidays.

Stage performers also introduced many dances that were copied and brought into general use. In 1794, John Durang, the first American dancer of note, made his stage debut in Philadelphia. And it is said that Durang's Hornpipe, a dance he choreographed and sometimes performed on a tightrope, remained popular among some folk dancers well into the 20th century.

Dick Crum, who for 20 years was associated with the Duquesne University Tamburitzans in Pittsburgh, first as a dancer and then as a choreographer and technical advisor, has said that ethnic dances "are things of beauty and as such they are now being preserved rather like other things are being preserved in museums."

As is the case with music and dance, painting, sculpture, illustration, and other *visual art forms* originating in Pennsylvania have enjoyed a symbiotic relationship with creators and consumers in other parts of the world.

In the early years of their education, Pennsylvania students are introduced to a painting by Benjamin West, "William Penn's Treaty with the Indians," painted in 1772. For many, this is the quintessential Pennsylvania painting by a Pennsylvania artist. But this Quaker artist owed much of his success to training and sophistication he acquired in Italy and Great Britain, the lands of his forefathers, where he brought about a revolution in historical painting. Another Pennsylvania artist who created lasting Pennsylvania iconography is Alexander Milne Calder. Born in Aberdeen, Scotland, Calder made Pennsylvania his home in 1868 and acquired the commission to create the tremendous decorative sculptural program for Philadelphia's City Hall. This project consumed most of his career; while executing it he supervised a small army of artisans and workmen bringing Old World skills to the job. Calder's best-known work probably is the gigantic statue of William Penn that

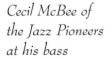

Cecil McBee of the Jazz Pioneers at his bass

stands on top of Philadelphia's City Hall. Based on Benjamin West's depiction of the state's founder, Calder's statue is 36 feet tall and weighs 26 tons. Calder passed on his artistic genius and innovative nature to his son, Alexander Stirling Calder, and to his grandson, Alexander Calder (with no middle name.)

The inter-cultural exchange that enriched the work of Benjamin West and Alexander Calder is even more pronounced in the story of another Pennsylvania artist, Mary Cassatt. Born of French heritage, in Allegheny City, now part of Pittsburgh, Cassatt spent her early years growing up in Philadelphia. She traveled throughout Pennsylvania and made many journeys to Europe. By the 1860s, she resolved to become an artist and enrolled in the Pennsylvania Academy of Fine Arts. After she mastered the simple copying methods taught there she went to France. Her friend and colleague Edgar Degas introduced her to the French Impressionists.

She quickly adopted their techniques, using a high-keyed palette and applying paint to her canvasses in small touches. She painted scenes from ordinary life like many of the painters she emulated with her own flourish of innovation. She exhibited with the French Impressionists from 1879 until 1886, but during that period developed her own specialty.

Because she was denied access to the café society enjoyed by her male peers and because she was responsible for the care of aging parents, she drew her subject matter from the home. Her parents, her sister, Lydia, and her nieces and nephews became frequent subjects. She was attracted to the theme of mothers with children, and painted it the rest of her life. Later she broke new ground in the art world by mastering the skill of Japanese print-making and incorporating the large, sharply silhouetted forms of the Japanese into her own manner of painting.

As Cassatt was evolving into one of the world's most respected Impressionist painters, another Pennsylvania artist was amassing a body of work that is singled out today as much for the striking simplicity of genius as for its ethnological significance. George Catlin was born in Wilkes-Barre, Luzerne County, and attended a classical school in that city. His teachers encouraged his interest in art history and he developed an interest in painting.

Eventually he moved to Philadelphia, where he painted portraits and miniatures. While he was in Philadelphia, a delegation of Plains Indians on their way to Washington visited the city and the sight of the entourage moved Catlin deeply. He saw in their bearing and deportment the classical ideals he had become acquainted with in his youth. He decided to record the appearance and manners of these Native Americans before their way of life disappeared. He went west and explored the countryside of the Missouri River, sketching and painting as he traveled, and then proceeded to the Southwest. Later he went to the Southeast.

Catlin completed nearly 500 paintings. He captured the essential distinctions—physical and cultural—among members of nearly 50 different tribes. With the detail he gave to clothing, headdresses, and other paraphernalia, he imbued these works with tremendous value for anthropologists as well as for collectors who saw a greatness that transcended historical usefulness.

English tastes in art, derived partly from Roman, Greek, Egyptian, and Byzantine traditions, dominated the early work of most Pennsylvania artists, but others, like Benjamin West and Mary Cassatt, left their own distinctive marks on the art world. West caused a revolution in history painting. Cassatt, in her later years, turned to the Orient, for an infusion of fresh vision that lifts us beyond nature while revealing our own natures. Such is the power of art, music, and dance.

City Hall, Philadelphia, carving, William Penn statue

In more recent times, another Pennsylvania painter, this time with family roots in Eastern Europe, made startling innovation an integral part of his artwork. Andy Warhol, born in Pittsburgh in 1928, took Pennsylvania to the front pages of art journals with controversial, distinct, and lasting contributions. Like Mary Cassatt, he worked with the most common images of his world. Warhol's images, however, struck the viewer with a commerciality that earned him both praise and criticism. He manipulated representations of Campbell soup cans, Brillo pads, and Coca-Cola bottles freely within the confines of the silkscreen process. He used images of celebrities like Marilyn Monroe and Jackie Kennedy boldly to express the conflict between immediacy and detachment, a preoccupation of the times in which he worked and one that is still debated today. After Warhol died in 1987, a museum, the largest one in the world dedicated to the work of one artist, opened in Pittsburgh.

In contrast to artists and illustrators like West and Warhol, Pennsylvania is home to innumerable artists who were not widely appreciated during their lifetimes but who made lasting contributions nevertheless. Lewis Miller, born in York in 1796, was a carpenter by trade but for 80 years he recorded the life and times of his family and his neighbor in amazing detail. His pen and ink sketches captured tradesmen, housewives, and children going about their everyday business long before photography could record their comings and goings. He sketched buildings and landscapes with the same exacting detail and, in many cases, his record of structures and people have been used to illuminate 19th century life in ways that could not have been achieved without his simplistic but sometimes brilliant views of Pennsylvania in the age before the camera.

Opera,
"Man of La Mancha",
Harrisburg Opera

During the same era, Jacob Maentel, born in Germany in 1763, made Pennsylvania his home. From about 1810 to 1825 he made simple portraits of Pennsylvania German country people with their proud bearing. Most of his figures are drawn in a flat silhouette form with the subject turned sideways. These figures often were placed on a rounded piece of land and almost always held something in their hands. Like many other self-taught artists his perspective is distorted, and in Maentel's work the distortion is considered part of the pieces charm and uniqueness. Sometime after 1825 he began to paint full-face portraits and moved to Indiana, where he died in or near his 100th year.

A legion of skilled and not-so-skilled artists who create *fraktur*, the German decorated lettering of texts, can be added to the roll call of enduring Pennsylvania artists who enriched the state's ethnic and universal value.

Women and children who painted, made samplers, pieced quilts, and designed clothing join the corps of creators who have given Pennsylvania a distinctive color, rhythm, exuberance, and joy. In many cases their identities are unknown, hidden, or incorporated into the overall pattern in an unobtrusive way.

In the broad picture of Pennsylvania's artistic heritage, the essence of Pennsylvania, its diversity of natural resources, is repeated again and again. Silhouettes of white oak trees and images of acorns show up on blanket chests, samplers, and tall-case clocks. Leaves, vines, and fruit are pierced into tin lanterns and etched onto the barrels of rifles. They are carved into bedposts, chair legs, and tabletops, and they decorate other useful products from redware to wrought iron. Fields of wheat, rye, and barley, the flow of water down a hillside, and the shadows of late afternoon inspire patterns on coverlets and quilts. In recent decades, many historical societies in Pennsylvania have carried on quilt documentation projects, and these activities will reveal distinctive qualities within regions of Pennsylvania and provide a better understanding of how regionalism is tied to ethnicity.

The names that Pennsylvania women give their quilts are testimony to the natural elements and lifestyles of the people around them. Among the favored patterns are "Log Cabin," "Flower Garden," "Tumbling Blocks," "Drunkard's Path," "Flying Geese," "Double Wedding Ring," and "Crazy Quilt." The diversity among Pennsylvania women and their art forms is also evident. The Amish quilters of Pennsylvania prefer large areas of plain fabric making up geometric patterns in plain reds, purples, blues, greens, and even browns, while women from other ethnic and religious communities use fabric printed with tiny flowers, stripes, and silhouettes.

Some believe that quilting began as a way of recycling small scraps of material from discarded clothing and fabric from other sources. Others believe this practice would not have been practical since differences in the degree of wear on each piece would have made the finished product subject to deterioration in uneven patterns. Quilts have gained new uses in recent years as modern generations acquire an appreciation for their beauty as well as usefulness. Interior decorators, for instance, are hanging them on walls of public buildings. Organizers of family reunions are piecing quilts and asking each family or individual who attends the annual get-together to sign a "block" within the quilt to document participation that particular year. Groups of quilters can be found in almost every community in Pennsylvania. Some groups work for charitable purposes, some for recreation, and others for family members who want to hold onto a tradition that seems to be fading right before their eyes.

Groups encouraging old art forms thrive in Pennsylvania, and even with the ever-increasing competition for leisure time, there are hundreds of art associations, craft guilds, singing groups, and dance ensembles that stimulate creativity and make Pennsylvania a major contributor to the arts of America and the world.

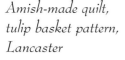
Amish-made quilt, tulip basket pattern, Lancaster

Artist
Benjamin West's
"Christ Healing",
Harmonists' collection

As homes, restaurants, hospitals, and other places display the visual arts in their many forms, the halls, theaters, and townhouses of Pennsylvania also bear witness to a wide variety of sounds transported to this land in the minds and arms of people settling here. Some of those people brought musical instruments and artists supplies where they might have carried more clothing or other personal effects.

Jovo Crljenicca, who was born near Karlovac, Croatia, in 1875, arrived in America with six tambura instruments under his arms. Many other immigrants also brought tambura instruments instead of their clothes. These people came to the United States from Serbia, a country that won its independence in 1878 at the Congress of Berlin. Serbia was rich with tamburitza music during this period and the Belgrade Choral Society was enjoying huge popularity.

The tamburitza takes its place alongside the bagpipe, usually associated with the Scottish and the Irish, the bouzouki, a Greek long-necked lute, and the balalaika, brought to Pennsylvania by Russian immigrants.

With the presence of Lutherans and Moravians and other groups that make music a part of their liturgy, it is understandable that Pennsylvania is known as the home of organ builders. David Tannenberg, born in 1728, learned his craft from Johann Klemm, a Moravian organ builder in Bethlehem. Following Klemm's death in 1762, Tannenberg moved to Lititz, where he began a 40-year career. He built more than 40 pipe organs, his last in 1804.

Pennsylvania's tradition continues. Today the state is home to the largest builder of church organs in the world. Jerome Markowitz founded the Allen Organ Company of Macungie, Lehigh County, and for more than 60 years the Markowitz family has managed the company with a long-term commitment to customer satisfaction. The company counts 75,000 installations in churches and synagogues throughout the world.

Pennsylvania is also home to one of the world's most famous guitar makers, the Martin Guitar Company of Nazareth, Northampton County. Like so many other Pennsylvania industries, this manufacturer also traces its roots to Germany. Christian Frederick Martin Sr., born in Markneukirchen, Germany, took up the family craft in 1796. At the age of 15, he left his hometown and traveled to Vienna to apprentice with Johann Stauffer, a renowned guitar maker. He mastered the skills, but because he believed trade guilds were restricting his business he sought out opportunities in Pennsylvania. By the 1830s he was operating a workshop in Nazareth, and eventually the workshop grew into a factory. Always attentive to consumer trends, the factory became known in the mid-1900s for its ukuleles. Today the sixth generation of the Martin family is operating the business.

In recent decades Pennsylvania's musical heritage has widened as the sitar and the tabla from India have taken their places alongside the organ, piano, accordion, banjo, tamburitza, bouzouki, balalaika, bagpipe, steel drum, and the drums of the Native Americans and of many African nations. The settings in which these musical forms are presented can range from the formal concert hall to the street corner, band shell, or the park gazebo. The costumes, hair dress, and accessories worn by presenters combine with the backdrop of indoor or outdoor settings. The participation of the audiences and the give-and-take of individual and group interpretation make up an experience characteristically Pennsylvanian. Together, they bring the dance, music, and the visual arts within reach of all who will pause to enjoy the richness and diversity of Pennsylvania today.

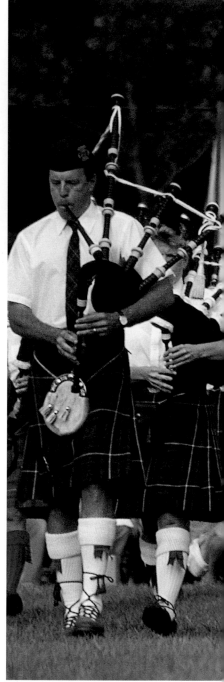

Above Left: *Bagpipers prepare for competition at the Ligonier Highland Games in Idlewood Park in Westmoreland County.* **Below Left:** *The kilted Southminster Ringers of Southminster Presbyterian Church in Mt. Lebanon, a Pittsburgh suburb, perform in the Scottish music tradition. Founded in 1969, these teen handbell ringers use bells up to the fifth octave.* **Above:** *Massed pipe bands parade at Ligonier. Since 1959, the Ligonier Highland Games have featured traditional Scottish cultural arts.* **Next Pages:** *Ballet Cultural Raices (Roots), a Lancaster County group dancing traditional numbers from the Dominican Republic, includes recent immigrants.*

CAMILLE ERICE

Passing on traditions from the Spanish-speaking nations became a compelling role for Camille Erice almost by accident. One day when she was about 5 years old, her family learned of a festival planned for her New York Harlem neighborhood. Her mother made her a dress like flamenco dancers wear, and Camille attended the event wearing her new finery and a self-confident smile.

"I didn't really know very much about flamenco at the time," she recalled, "but wearing that dress and taking in the reactions of people around me gave me such joy. It made me wonder what flamenco dancers feel like when they are dancing. I became very interested in the dance and the culture."

Camille Erice, founder of Danzante, teaches Flamenco dance

Today Camille is executive director of Danzante, a thriving Latino arts and cultural organization she and flamenco guitarist Paco Molinero started. The group's home is in the newly-renovated McFarland Building in inner-city Harrisburg with three dance studios with wooden floors, a small theater, art room, library/computer lab, locker rooms, gallery and reception area, and three offices. Artists from all disciplines work with young people and their families teaching flamenco dance, fine art, Latin percussion, photography, theater, and other arts after-school and on Saturday afternoons.

Although Danzante is an archaic Spanish word meaning "dancer," to educators and community leaders Danzante, the organization, is much more than a dancer. They turn to Camille and the artists to enhance their arts-in-education and community outreach programs. Danzante sponsors a summer arts camp that has brought in artists from many countries and throughout the United States. It is well known throughout the region for its dazzling and exciting interpretations of flamenco dance.

For Camille and her artists, practice is the key to success. On a typical afternoon the wooden floors in her studios reverberate with strong rhythmic music as Camille and others work with adults and children ages 6 and up, teaching them the dances their great-grandmothers and great-grandfathers might have danced in the Spanish-speaking countries.

"Move in a little," she instructs a group of students assuming the classic flamenco posture. "I want to see everyone straightening out, and let's see nice smiles." She adjusts the hand position on the waist of one of the young ladies. Directing her attention to the boys she demonstrates, "You know the men keep their fingers together and feet like this."

Geoffrey Weeks begins strumming a flamenco song and Camille leads a passionate, self-confident choreography that sets hearts beating faster. For a girl who always wanted to be a teacher and dancer, this is a dream come true.

While growing up, Camille did not have the opportunities and a community art center like the one that she has established. "Youth is so precious," Camille believes. "Children need continuity in their lives, a place they can go to and feel safe with caring adults. They need to know that they can be what they want to be; that the more you work on something, the better you become at it; that instant gratification is not good, but hard work is; that they can all be something very special."

Camille's life achievements also include motherhood: a son and daughter and three grandchildren. Like most girls in her neighborhood, Camille married at an early age and worked hard to raise her children with little support. She divorced her husband and soon

Camille Erice

after met Molinero. The accomplished flamenco guitarist fascinated Camille and they decided to go to Spain so she could follow her dream of studying flamenco dance. They immersed themselves in Spanish culture, dance, and music. She studied with some of the masters as Paco played for the classes, and she returned to the United States with a fresh vision and renewed energy.

Camille and Paco moved to Perry County, where a group of artists, formerly from Philadelphia, had settled and become a vital part of the community, creating many festivals and musical gatherings. The early meetings of the Perry County Council on the Arts were in her kitchen. In 1978, Camille discovered that the Harrisburg YWCA had a studio with wooden floors and she asked about its availability. The YWCA told her that she could use the studio free if she taught flamenco classes, and that was the beginning of Danzante.

In the early 1980s, the YWCA closed the dance studio and Camille had to find another location. She was able to work out an arrangement with the First Church of the Brethren to use their stage free if she again taught dance to neighborhood children. This started Danzante's work with community children and also established the fact that children in the community had no place to develop their creative talents and abilities. In the 1980s and through the 1990s, Camille and Paco taught Spanish dance to many community children weekly at the church. Other artists who wanted to share their talents with the children joined them.

Tanya Ortiz brought theater classes. Ricardo Kearns, an accomplished poet and journalist, taught poetry and literature. In 1992, Camille and a group of Danzante aficionados got together because of their concern about issues plaguing youth in the community and incorporated Danzante as a non-profit to obtain funding to increase its arts programs. With funding established, Camille was able to hire additional artists to enhance opportunities for community children.

While Camille was teaching dance and developing Danzante, she also worked full-time as a human development educator for Planned Parenthood, a children and family health care and nutrition administrator with Hamilton Health Center, and with the City of Harrisburg as a human relations representative dealing with civil rights issues. She has served on numerous non-profit boards including the Community Action Commission, Dauphin County Children and Youth Advisory Council, Children's Playroom, and Harrisburg Area Community College's Multi-Cultural Advisory Committee.

Camille, with Paco's encouragement, developed a scholarship fund so that students who demonstrate exemplary talent in dance can forward their career as a dancer/choreographer. Dileiby Saez, a student of Camille's since age 8, was sent to the University of New Mexico's Flamenco Institute for three consecutive years. Today Dileiby heads Danzante's Flamenco Dance Program as teacher and choreographer.

On the long path to success, Camille's hard work paid off. She has won many local, regional, and statewide honors, but as an accomplished flamenco dancer and art center administrator she prefers to stay focused on the dance rather than accolades.

In 1992, Camille married Kevin Novinger, businessman and co-founder of the Perry County Council of the Arts. Kevin volunteers on Danzante's board and has been involved in all its fund-raising activities since its incorporation in 1992.

"Dance is mostly hard work, but the rewards are endless," she tells her students. "Practice makes perfect."

Above: *Greek food festivals sponsored by Greek Orthodox churches across the state often include dance performances enjoyed by the community. Males at a Harrisburg festival show their machismo while the girls watch from the sidelines.* **Above Right:** *The girls perform a solo part in the* anatolitiko, *a dance from Eastern Asia Minor.* **Below Right:** *Dancers of the Holy Trinity Cathedral, Camp Hill, the Junior Olympic Flames, dance a* syrtaki, *which is similar to the dance of* pendozali *from the island of Crete.*

Above Left: *The most often performed Lebanese dance is the depka. These Lebanese perform at the Pittsburgh Folk Festival, an annual event begun in 1956 to spotlight the cultural arts of the ethnic groups that settled in this city.* **Below Left:** *At the Polish Festival in Philadelphia, the PKM Dancers perform at Penn's Landing. Music groups play and Polish food is served at the festival.* **Above:** *The Pirin Bulgarian National Folk Ensemble performs national dances at the F. M. Kirby Center, Wilkes-Barre.*

Above: *Since 1937, Pittsburgh's Duquesne University has been home for the Tamburitzans, a performing folk ensemble that perpetuates cultures of eastern Europe.* **Above Right:** *Wearing embroidered bodices and headpieces with flowing ribbons, a Ukrainian group dances at the Pittsburgh Folk Festival. Their costumes are hand-woven, their skirts and vests of wool and the blouses and aprons of linen.* **Below Right:** *Lithuanians show the dress, rhythm, and steps of a traditional folk dance.*

Previous Pages: *A harvest dance organized by the Polish Youth Organization brought familiar music, steps, and costumes to attendees at a Polish festival at Our Lady of Czestochowa Shrine, Doylestown.* **Left:** *The Junior Tamburitzans perform at the Pittsburgh Folk Festival.* **Below:** *Enthusiastic Lithuanian dancers take a bow at a national festival devoted to their heritage at Barnesville.*

Left: *Kazka, a Ukrainian dance ensemble led by P. A. Duda, a Kutztown University professor, dances a polka at Patch Town Days, Eckley Miners' Village, Eckley.* **Below Left:** *Youth from Lester Miller and the Country Folks do hoedowning and jigging at the Kutztown Pennsylvania German Festival.* **Below:** *Precision clogging, here at a street fair in Marietta, is dancing according to prescribed routines with the feet very close to the ground except for high kicks. Cloggers often wear shoes with "jingle" taps on their heels and soles. A dance style famed in Appalachia from southern Pennsylvania to northern Georgia, clogging has roots in steps danced by Cherokee Indians, slaves from Africa, and English and Irish immigrants.*

Below: *With ethnic ties to Slovenia, a mountainous area bordering the Adriatic Sea within the Balkans, accordion players of the Slovenia Heritage Association have performed throughout the U.S. and Canada. Immigrants from Slovenia have traditionally set up "button box clubs" to play accordion music in America.* **Right:** *Children perform energetic dance steps at the Pittsburgh Folk Festival.*

Left, Below and Below Right: *Utilizing three stages and large exhibition rooms the Pittsburgh Folk Festival, under the banner "Unity in Diversity," boasts continuous entertainment for three days annually over Memorial Day weekend. More than 20 nationalities as diverse as Ukraine, Greece, Philippines, Vietnam, China, and Scotland set up art booths, play ethnic games, demonstrate craft skills, and dance, dance, dance. For more than 40 years, Pittsburgh's ethnic communities have come together at the festival to revel in one another's traditions. In their national costumes, the dancers and musician on these pages delight in showing off their heritage.*

Above: *The late Arthur Hall, a Philadelphian, established a dance ensemble to honor the artistic heritage of the African diaspora in Pennsylvania.* **Right:** *This costume, worn at an ethnic celebration in front of Pennsylvania's Capitol, combines African royalty and African-American creativity.* **Next Pages**: *Teaching African-style dances nurtures appreciation within African-Americans for their cultural roots.*

Left: *The sitar, an Indian instrument, is featured at a workshop conducted by famed Indian musician, Shafaatullah Khan, at the arts festival at Little Buffalo State Park, Perry County.* **Above:** *A Chinese dancer gracefully swirls a scarf to add to the beauty of her own body movements.*

Above: *Women of Philippine descent dance the world-renowned tinikling, which calls for clacking of bamboo poles, usually in 3/4 time, with dancers moving their feet to avoid any collision.*
Right: *Mountain tribes from northern Luzon contributed this dance of balancing pots to the national culture of the Philippines, a country of islands with close ties to the U.S.*

Left: *David and Melissa Marks handcraft and play dulcimers and other Old World instruments, here at the Kutztown Pennsylvania German Festival, where they have exhibited more than 20 years.* **Top:** *An Erie group performs a dance of northern Greece called thrace.* **Above:** *Musikfreunde Geretshausen, a woodwind ensemble from Germany, performs at Bethlehem Musikfest, an annual nine-day marathon of hundreds of varied music performances.*

Above: *Linda E. Brubaker demonstrates theorem painting, an art taught from 1810 to 1830 at Linden Hall, a girls' school in Lititz started by Moravians.* **Right:** *Bun Em, a silk weaver who immigrated to Pennsylvania from Cambodia, was awarded a National Heritage Fellowship in 1990 for mastering an art from her tradition.* **Next Pages:** *The early art of German immigrants adorned utilitarian objects such as this painted 1774 chest. It is draped by an 1837 handwoven blanket. Both are on exhibit at The Historical Society of Berks County, Reading.*

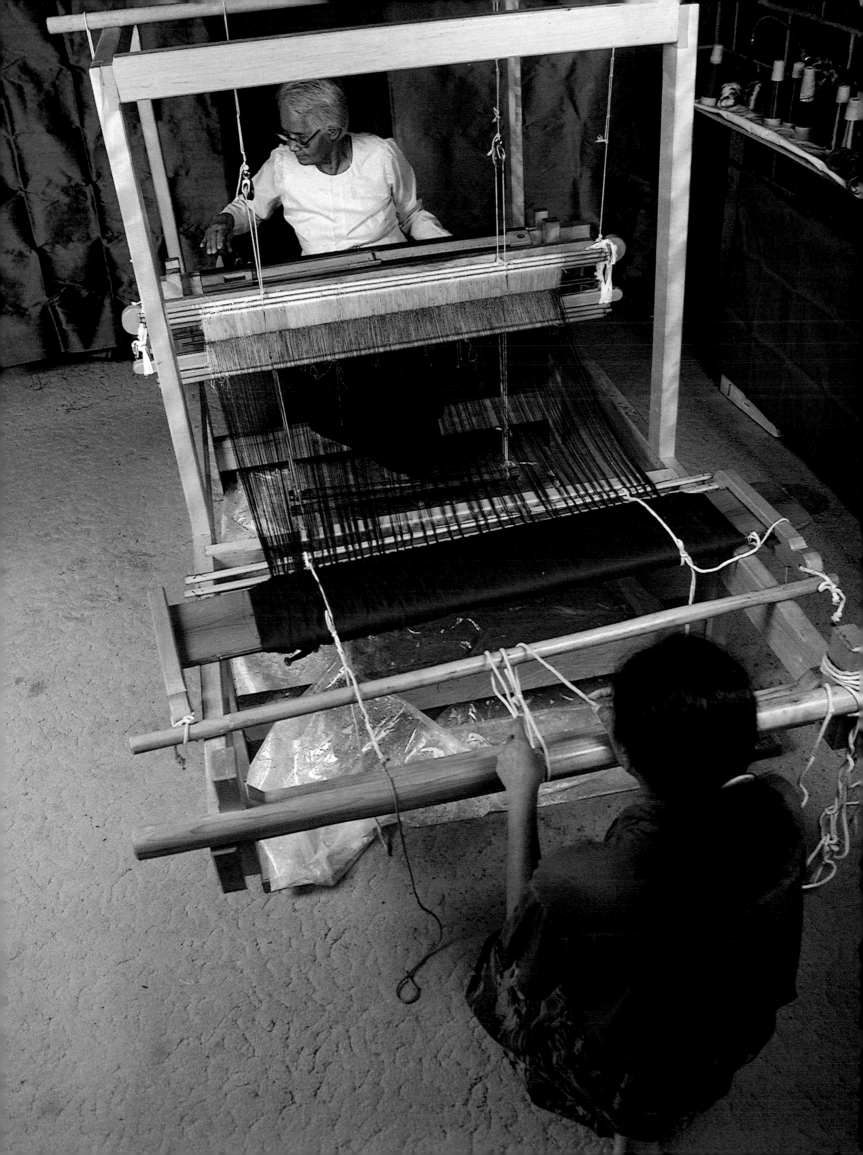

Left: *A Ukrainian family displays its prized collection of pysanky eggs made by several generations of family members.* **Above:** *An African-American quilt with motifs such as masks and fertility images made by Sandra Godfrey is exhibited at a folk festival. While Amish-made quilts usually use solid unprinted patterns, quilts of other ethnic groups employ patterns, artwork, and writing on their quilts.*

Above: *Samplers made by local Mennonites from 1819-1825 are displayed at the Mennonite Heritage Meetinghouse, a museum of Mennonite German culture and faith, in Montgomery County.* **Right:** *Also at the Meetinghouse is an exhibit of books showing* fraktur, *a German art motif.* **Next Pages:** *An Amish-made quilt illustrates the simplicity of their solid color designs.*

Below: J. Ketner of Berks Co. sands the wooden runner of a traditional sled that he makes at his Oley Sledworks. Bottom: Visitor Michael DelBonifro examines a carving in the display by Fooks Woodworks at the State Craft Fair held at Franklin & Marshall College, Lancaster. Right: Diane Myers, a member of the Pennsylvania Guild of Craftsmen from Jersey Shore, demonstrates the techniques of making handcrafted baskets.

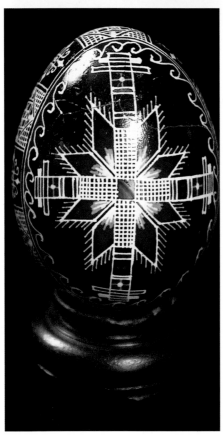

These early artworks are from the extensive German-American collection of Dr. David Bronstein. **Top Left:** *Painted wood dogs were carved by well-known Pennsylvania German artist Wilhelm Schimmel.* **Left:** *This 1772 painted blanket chest made for Ann Maria Trexler illustrates the exuberance of German decoration.* **Far Left:** *Ukrainian egg designs are included in the collection.* **Below:** *A Jacob Maentel painting that is distinguished by side profiles sits on the chair rail below an example of early style fraktur. The cupboard exhibits German painted boxes and Schimmel carvings, and the clock is an example of the best in craftsmanship.*

chapter three

When people first arrived in what is now Pennsylvania, they found an abundance of natural resources. The earliest Europeans came from lands that had been nearly depleted of timber, and some came from areas where water already was scarce or polluted because of the early industrial development that had taken place.

The earliest settlers brought few tools with them and in most cases the utensils needed for daily life were fashioned from the materials at hand: wood, clay, furs, and grasses. The English and Welsh who settled here in the days of William Penn benefited to a small degree from earlier habitation by the Swedes, Dutch, and Finns, but building shelter and establishing small gardens took precedence over plying trades

OLD WORLD ARTISANS

Benjamin Rittenhouse clock, 1700's, Montgomery County Historical Society collection

learned in the old country. In many cases, the first builders of homes, stables, barns, and smokehouses were not experienced in the building trades. Sharing skills with neighbors, relatives, and friends became as common as sharing food, clothing, and the other necessities of life.

A pioneer's best friends were his axe and his rifle, and these basic tools helped the earliest generations to establish a homestead and furnish it. A few of the earliest settlers, like Francis Daniel Pastorius, lived temporarily in caves when they first arrived. Most fashioned huts from wood, branches, twigs, animal hair, and sometimes mud. They made containers like pots and plates from wood or the clay available in many areas where they worked. Blending skills they learned in the Old World with skills they learned from the Native Americans, they built Pennsylvania in an image that spanned Old World ideas and New World reality.

Conestoga wagon displayed at the State Museum, Harrisburg

Within a few decades Pennsylvania's early settlers were making items distinctively Pennsylvania in nature, feel, and use. From the late 18th and early 19th centuries, the Pennsylvania rifle and the Conestoga wagon are the most remarkable of the early artisans' work. Eventually, skilled artisans plied their trades in the early settlements like New Sweden, Germantown, and Philadelphia. As competition and opportunity grew, they ventured into the frontier, where their skills were much in demand.

In general, the English-speaking settlers, interested in trade and commerce, remained in the cities and towns. Naturally, Philadelphia became their chief center of influence, but they were also present in the far reaches of the colony. Some became merchants, worked in government offices, or established shops where they sold things they made such as furniture and household goods. A few offered imported goods, but these items were costly and only the wealthiest could afford products made on the Old Continent.

The Germans who followed the first waves of English and Welsh arrived in great numbers. Many of those arriving from the regions along the Rhine River in Western Europe found the cities and towns in America too noisy, dirty, or congested. After a brief stay in a coastal town, they moved into rural areas west and north of the English settlements and became trappers, traders, farmers, and scouts, often allied with Quakers in business and social interchange. German-speaking people were also found in iron forges and furnaces and bloomeries, built in many cases with English capital and operated by English overseers. This fact is evident today in some of the products that have survived. Germans working for English-speaking proprietors decorated the sides of early stoves with images from the German culture and with Biblical verses or proverbs spelled out in the German language. English entrepreneurs also set up mills on nearly every stream and creek in the southeastern region of Pennsylvania and employed Germans as laborers paid by the hour or day. By 1790, approximately one-third of the Pennsylvania population was of German extraction.

Out of necessity, the earliest farmers applied or learned the skills of carpenters and blacksmiths to keep their farm in operation. Later, tailors, shoemakers, candlemakers, weavers, bakers, butchers, and many other tradesmen found a ready market for their skills.

At that time almost one-third of the population was made up of Scotch-Irish people moving here from Northern Ireland. But many other ethnic groups were represented here too. Of all the colonies before the Revolution, Pennsylvania had the greatest diversity in ethnic make-up. Small numbers of Swedes, Dutch, Finns, French, Native Americans, and Africans contributed to the Pennsylvania population from the earliest days of European settlement.

Anthony Johnson, one of 20 Africans brought to this country as slaves in 1619, was freed in 1622 or 1623, so the migration of blacks to Pennsylvania may have preceded the days of William Penn. After the Civil War, of course, migration of blacks to Pennsylvania increased from a trickle in the early days of colonization to a vast wave that is still ebbing and waning today.

In 1688 a group of Mennonites and Quakers from Germantown presented a petition to the Pennsylvania assembly urging the abolition of slavery, and in 1754 the Philadelphia Yearly Meeting of Quakers condemned slavery. Many Quakers freed the slaves they held in response to this declaration. At the opening of the Revolutionary War, 6,000 slaves lived in Pennsylvania. Slavery was not profitable under the economic system and in February 1780 the Pennsylvania legislature passed an abolition bill by a vote of 34 to 21. This made Pennsylvania the first state to abolish slavery by an act of legislation. The act declared that children born to slave mothers were free, but some of their parents served as slaves well into the 18th century.

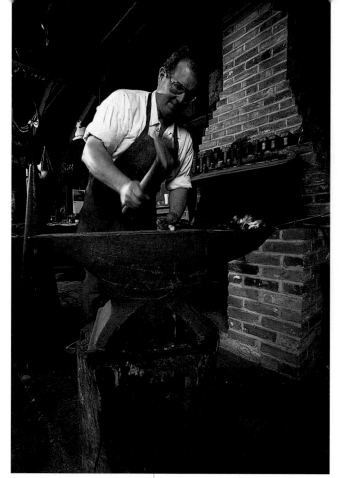

*Blacksmith
Bob Hanson at
Mill Creek Village,
Lancaster County*

While slaves and freed blacks worked at mostly domestic jobs in Pennsylvania for many years to come, a few of the freed blacks became successful business people. In general, the freed blacks stayed in large cities and towns for reasons pertaining to safety and culture. One of the exceptions to this generalization was William Goodridge. Goodridge was born to a slave in Maryland and sent to York, Pennsylvania, when still a lad to apprentice with a tanner. In about 1821 he opened a barbershop in York and, with the help of his wife, Emily, nurtured the business until it became a large emporium offering exotic wares from oranges and lemons to perfumes and daily newspapers. Goodridge was one of the first to make ambrotypes, a precursor to modern-day photographs.

Arriving here after dealing with harsh conditions in their homeland, the Irish were ambitious and adapted well to frontier conditions. Many moved westward, carving out the frontier with others compelled by opportunity. Many became laborers. They built turnpikes and bridges, dug canals, and laid track for the railroads. These transportation routes opened up new markets and for many decades there seemed to be no end to the need for large numbers of men and boys to work on public and private projects. Eventually the coal mines, the oil industry, and the steel plants employed many newcomers, and owners of these large industries soon found themselves with a diverse work force where many languages and cultures came together.

Women and girls, whether town dwellers or farm folk, developed many cottage industries, like making clothes to sell to neighbors or producing butter, bread, or smoked meats for sale at public markets. The female population was largely responsible for making cloth, fabricating clothes, and keeping fires for cooking and heating and many other laborious chores. In many cases, the females also nurtured kitchen gardens, and tended chickens, milk cows, sheep, goats, and other domestic animals. They also helped in raising wheat, barley, rye, corn, and buckwheat.

When winters forced everyone indoors, there was repair work to do in the home, the barn, and the shop. In the towns and cities, one-person shops turned into stores that sold numerous items. Businesses providing services such as bookbinding, clock making, and printing opened. Taverns and inns sprang up at nearly every crossroad and intersection.

When the Industrial Revolution swept through America after 1838, the workers of Pennsylvania quickly made the state a leader in production of goods and services.

The Fortney family, French Huguenots who migrated from Western Europe after a brief stay in Holland, traded expertise in making Pennsylvania rifles among other Huguenots spread out across Pennsylvania and into other states where natural migration westward took them. One gunsmith, Melchior Fordney, operated a shop in Lancaster and helped brothers, cousins, and other family members operating shops in York and other towns. Fordney was descended from the Fortineux family who arrived in Pennsylvania in the 1730s. Not surprisingly, the family name today is spelled many ways, ranging from Fortune to Fordney and Fortney to Fortna.

At the age of 18, Melchior was apprenticed to his gunsmith brother-in-law Abraham Switzer. Melchior's carving and engraving work are considered among the best produced by Pennsylvania artisans of the late 18th and early 19th centuries, but numerous relatives and associates claim excellence in other areas of this trade and related trades such as clock making and the engraving of money and notes.

Because woodworking skills were needed in gunsmithing, clock making, wagon making, and many other small industries, the exchange among artisans fostered cooperation and fueled the barter system, just as it did in trades that involved natural resources such as iron ore, clay, stone, and harvest from gardens and fields.

Jews came to Pennsylvania in small numbers at first. Later, large waves of migration brought them to Pennsylvania from mostly middle and eastern European regions. Nevertheless, by the 1730s practicing Jews had already settled in Philadelphia, Easton, Lancaster, Heidelberg (Schafferstown), Pittsburgh, and other towns. Jewish communities like those in Lancaster, Schaefferstown, York, and Hanover were small and sometimes disappeared with the departure of just a few families. About 100 Jews lived in Philadelphia during the early period of Jewish settlement. But this number expanded to more than 1,000 in just a few years. Among them were brothers Bernard and Michael Gratz, who came to Pennsylvania from Upper Silesia in central Europe and founded one of the most successful mercantile houses of colonial America.

Partially, because non-Christians were excluded from holding public office in Pennsylvania through the middle of the 18th century, Jewish businessmen in places like Baltimore and New York worked in Pennsylvania through agents like Joseph Simon, a successful figure in the Lancaster community. Eventually Jews were licensed to trade with the Indians, or they became peddlers, carrying their wares from town to town in Pennsylvania as they did in other places. Some peddlers collected scraps of cloth and other discarded items and exchanged them for cash at places where they were needed. Paper mills, one of Pennsylvania's earliest industrial sites, had an insatiable need for rags before the use of wood pulp as the key ingredient in the paper making business.

German Jews felt at home among Pennsylvania's German-speaking population and among their Jewish brethren in Philadelphia, Pittsburgh, and Harrisburg. To gain legitimacy and respect, the Jewish community in Germany had demonstrated its members' willingness to become good Germans. They carried this attribution with them to the United States and it thrust them into civic affairs and public charities. As migration continued, Jewish people put down communities in Reading, Pottsville, Wilkes-Barre, Scranton, Erie, Allentown, Danville, and Honesdale. By 1870, most medium-sized towns had, at the least, a legal congregation (10 men) of German Jews. As the German Jews became upwardly mobile and more influential in Pennsylvania, a wave of Jews from the Russian empire arrived as a result of the anti-Semitic movement beginning in 1881 and lasting through 1914.

Between 1889 and 1910, approximately 100,000 eastern European Jews migrated to Pennsylvania. Old communities were enlarged and new ones were formed. In the mid-1920s, when the immigration period ended, more that 300,000 Jews lived in Pennsylvania.

Because earlier settlers had taken positions in retail stores, the new immigrants took jobs as peddlers in the small communities of Pennsylvania or worked in the gritty shops of larger cities. Some were employed by iron and steel companies to manage the company store since their facility with languages allowed them to communicate with the workers who had come from familiar regions. But as peddlers and laborers worked hard, saved, and improved their lot in the New World, some became owners of factories and workshops. One industry in which the Jews stood out was the cigar manufacturing business.

In Pittsburgh and Philadelphia, "the stogey trade" was considered a Jewish industry and other cities like Lancaster and York also had a large workforce in this industry. With ties to New York City's garment industry, many Jewish business owners opened factories in the towns and cities of Pennsylvania, attracting immigrants from the American South as opportunities in road building, mining, farming, and public projects dwindled.

Decor hinges, 1740-41, Moravian Museum collection

Another group that swelled Pennsylvania's population was the Italians. From the time of the Revolutionary War until about 1880, Italian migration to Pennsylvania reflected changing economic, political, and social conditions. Philadelphia was the destination for most Italians in the antebellum period, with most migrating from northern provinces of Italy. They were well educated and prominent in their trades and professions. For example, Filippo Traeta, a musician and composer, came to Philadelphia and established a music conservatory. Although many of the Italians who took up residence in Philadelphia were musicians and artists whose stay was temporary, some came to the city permanently to further their economic status or to enjoy greater political freedom. These immigrants came to Philadelphia with their families, an indication of their intention to stay.

In later years many factors in the Italian regions brought immigrants to Pennsylvania, setting the stage for the second and most important immigration, between 1880 and the outbreak of World War I. Some were agricultural laborers, but many were familiar with the wage system of labor. Many came from the southern regions of Italy during this period, bringing vast differences in culture and heritage easily stereotyped and characterized by others who preceded them from other regions.

Between 1870 and 1914, jobs were plentiful in growing American cities such as Philadelphia and Pittsburgh, and Italians who migrated to these cities worked at many different jobs before settling into one. Some had agricultural backgrounds and moved to areas where Pennsylvania's fertile soils provided rich rewards for labor and know-how. In the towns and villages, some worked as barbers, tailors, garment makers, hat makers, goldsmiths,

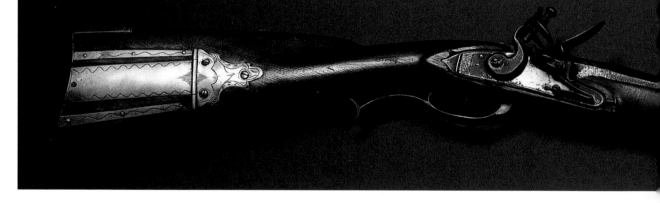

Pennsylvania rifle, 1700's, Fort Pitt Museum collection

shoemakers, masons, bricklayers, plumbers, carpenters, and stonecutters. In the 1880s, for example, Italian stonecutters began to migrate to the Easton area. Thousands worked in jobs that were low paying and hazardous, prompting them to support the labor union movement. Others, like Marcus Aurelius Renzetti, found jobs as sculptors and teachers.

Born in Abuzzi, Italy, Renzetti was a boy when his family moved to America. Settling just south of Philadelphia, Renzetti discovered his artistic talents early in life and earned a scholarship to the Pennsylvania Academy of Fine Arts. His career flourished. He found work in a commercial firm that produced statues for churches, and produced his own sculpture and ceramics. He joined the faculty at the Philadelphia Museum College of Art, where he nurtured talents for more than 30 years. His son, Peter, profiled in this book, became a master in ironwork and worked with the firm founded by Samuel Yellin, a Polish immigrant who established a metalworking shop on Arch Street in Philadelphia.

Italian artisans have left their mark throughout Pennsylvania. In 1930 Italian stoneworkers were employed to build St. Patrick's Church in Wilkes-Barre using marble cut in Italy, crated, and transported to Pennsylvania. At the same time, Italian artisans like

*Cigar making display,
Burgess Foulke
House, Quakertown*

Frank Vittor, born in Mozzato, Italy, were creating long-lasting works of art in the Pittsburgh area. Vittor became known as the "sculptor of presidents," creating busts of Calvin Coolidge, Woodrow Wilson, and Theodore Roosevelt. Perhaps his best-known work is the heroic-sized statue of Christopher Columbus that stands in Pittsburgh's Schenley Park.

Much like the English, the Irish, the Italians, and other ethnic groups in Pennsylvania, the Poles were influential in the early days of the state and became more numerous during the period of vast immigration in the late 1800s and early 1900s. Approximately two-and-one-half million Poles came to America from 1850 to 1914, first from German-controlled and then from Austrian-controlled, and finally from Russian-dominated lands. The main Polish settlements in Pennsylvania were in the anthracite coal regions found in Schuylkill County, the Wyoming Valley, Wilkes-Barre, and Scranton. Other Poles headed for the iron and steel centers and the bituminous coal towns of western Pennsylvania. Still others settled in Philadelphia and Erie. As with many other ethnic groups, second and third generation Poles gave steady support to the organization and strike efforts of the United Mine Workers (UMW) in the anthracite regions and to the Steel Workers Organizing Committee in steel plants of the Pittsburgh region.

Better wages in second and third generation families often enabled parents belonging to most ethnic groups to provide higher education for some of their children. Others moved to non-industrial and white-collar occupations. Migration of ethnic groups to Pennsylvania after World War I was minimal but plenty of notable exceptions exist. The influx of Asian peoples after the Korean and Vietnam wars furthered Pennsylvania's rich climate of diversity, and many of these people found work in restaurants and hotels as well as in factories, stores, and farm operations. Once again adverse conditions in the homelands became stimuli for people to excel in the United States. While many groups concentrated on assimilation in the mainstream of society, they kept traditions alive at home and in the place of worship. Some opened schools to teach, preserve, and nurture language, history, and tradition, while others tutored children in the languages and culture of their new homes, only to return to tradition in succeeding generations.

Within the United States itself, migration forces have changed the nature of Pennsylvania continually. During the years of World War II, many families living in rural areas of the south and west came to Pennsylvania, where employers heralded opportunities for better jobs and better lifestyles. Many African-Americans moved north. Some descendants of Pennsylvania Germans who had moved into the Shenandoah and Monongahela Valley areas returned to the lands settled by their forefathers, and a cycle of push and pull continued as people moved where opportunities beckoned.

In this mix of cultural, religious, and ethnic diversity, the constant and familiar element of change rings loud and clear.

Next Pages: *After researching the vanished art of Pennsylvania German redware potters, in 1898 Henry Chapman Mercer set up his Moravian Pottery and Tile Works in Doylestown, where he crafted, glazed, and baked clay tiles. Ornamental tiles like these that tell stories about The New World fascinated Mercer, who supported the arts and crafts movement. His patented tile-making continues at the Tile Works today.*

PETER A. RENZETTI

Old World craftsmanship and the cycle of nature go hand-in-hand in the workshop where Peter A. Renzetti produces museum-quality lighting fixtures, gates, furniture, and other hardware in his metalworking forge at Dilworthtown, Chester County. Clients from Pennsylvania to California call on his expertise and talents.

The Smithsonian Institution, National Park Service, and Winterthur Museum are a few of the many institutions that have commissioned him for consulting, designing, forging, sculpting, restoration, and *repoussé* work. (The latter term is French, meaning, "to push out from behind"—ultimately, to work a flat sheet of material into a three-dimensional form.) His work for individuals ranges from repairing an old lock to building entrance gates and foyer ornaments for the rich and famous.

A third generation Italian, Renzetti brings integrity to each job, reflecting his own heritage and the heritage of other craftsmen whose work he has examined, admired and, in many cases, restored. He believes that when he enters into a contract, the relationship he establishes with the client is just as important as the product and services commissioned. Interpreting the client's needs and deciding how to make the desired product functional, aesthetically pleasing, and cost-effective are points uppermost in his mind. These two sides of his business, however, are enhanced by a third concern—finishing the job on time and without mistakes.

Renzetti was born and reared in the arts and crafts community of Arden, Delaware, just a few miles from his present day forge. His father was an artist, sculptor, and teacher, and his mother a painter and illustrator. The town where he grew up had artists' studios and craft shops of many kinds, including a forge that operated from about 1914 through 1936. The craft shop eventually became apartments, but all the forge tools, patterns, and samples were put in storage.

Peter's father, Aurelius, loved to take him to school while he was teaching and included him in the classes. This exposed Peter to sculpture, drawing, carving, pottery, and working metals. As Peter grew older, he was allowed to roam the school and sit in on other classes that interested him, which laid the foundation for his interest in arts and crafts.

Renzetti enrolled in the vocational and industrial arts programs in high school. He attended the Kutztown Folk Festival in 1958 and became fascinated by the work of a blacksmith there. A friend gave him an anvil for his 16th birthday, and he started to teach himself blacksmithing.

For years he worked at silver and goldsmithing, carving in wood, and in welding and fabricating. He tried his hand at forging, at tool and die work, stone cutting, and industrial-scale model building. When he heard the craft shop with the Arden Forge in his hometown was being sold, he offered to buy the inventory and tools, and then began to look for a place where he could open his own forge. He found a place in nearby Chadds Ford, Pennsylvania, and opened his shop in 1970.

Peter specialized in the restoration and reproduction of historical hardware and ironwork and soon developed a clientele that included the Hagley Museum of Industry and the Metropolitan Museum of Art. Along the way he developed liaisons with architects, historical societies, and antique dealers. In 1975 he purchased the old James Dilworth

Blacksmith Shop, house, and log cabin. He moved his workshop to Dilworthtown, not far from Chadds Ford, and restored the buildings. He and his small staff became known for their reproduction work, and special clients called upon them many times for their restoration skill. Renzetti also bought, salvaged, and restored antique iron and hardware for resale.

In 1992 he entered a creative partnership with Samuel Yellin Metalworkers in Philadelphia and eventually moved that business into his workshop. Clare Yellin, granddaughter of firm founder Samuel Yellin, formed a team of craftspeople that includes Vic Pisani, Chris Tierney, and Alex Klahm of Alex Klahm Metalwork and Design of Florida. Workers today use machines, tools, and traditional techniques, and marry them with imagination, good design, and hand skills.

Renzetti's grandfather, "Vito," a tailor, came to the United States from Italy right after the turn of the century to make a better life for his family. Peter's father, Aurelius, was six years old at the time, and as he grew he exhibited a natural talent for the arts and was assisted by his father to pursue these talents. In his early teens he exhibited extraordinary skill as a sculptor. He enrolled at the Pennsylvania Academy of Fine Arts and won two Cresson Scholarships, in 1919 and 1922, to study abroad. He also started the Philadelphia Statuary Company that specialized in production plaster castings of sculptures, lamps, and various art forms. He developed a keen sense of what it takes to pass on skills to the next generation. Renzetti's father eventually became a teacher at the Philadelphia Museum School of Industrial Art, where he taught from 1930 to 1967. He also became active in the Samuel Fleischer Art Memorial, also known as the Graphic Sketch Club.

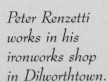

Peter Renzetti works in his ironworks shop in Dilworthtown.

After finishing the tenth grade in high school, Peter won a scholarship and enrolled in a machinist and tool die-making program at the Williamson Trade School in Media, graduating in 1962.

Peter gets great satisfaction out of working with other craftspeople. "We've lost something important as we have phased out the old bartering system," Renzetti offers. "Under the barter system, people in the crafts shared their skills with like-minded people and everyone benefited from the relationships formed." For the same reason, Renzetti believes that America lost an important link between learning and doing when the apprenticeship system declined.

"The exchange among craftsmen in all areas of work is vital to the growth and inspiration of artists and craftsmen and the education of the general public," he believes. "It's crucial that the craftsperson pass on the lessons he or she has learned from another person. Passing on something of what you have learned is as important as producing work that will stand the test of time."

A person does not always have the opportunity to give back to the same person who shared information, in Renzetti's view, but it is important to share it with someone else down the line.

"By passing on what we've learned from others," he theorizes, "we keep the cycle of nature turning. That is my theory of how the world of arts and crafts should work. You can call it the 'Renzetti Theory of Relativity!'"

Left: *Molten metal casting utilized Pennsylvania's natural resources and skills brought by European immigrants who settled before the machinery boom of the 19th century's Industrial Revolution.* **Top Left:** *A storefront window displays ironworks and stoneware relics to recall the town's history during a Danville festival.* **Above:** *Stonemasons cut the stones used in the grand staircase in the Rotunda of the state Capitol.*

Left: *Fine Philadelphia-made furniture—a walnut slant-front desk c.1700, with a walnut easy chair with wool damask upholstery c.1740, and Queen Anne brass and wrought-iron andirons— adorn Wright's Ferry Mansion, Columbia, a home that was at the edge of the frontier in 1738. The early Georgian paneling reflects luxury but less sophistication than the workmanship in many early 18th century Philadelphia homes.* **Below Left:** *Textile weaving was a valued skill that is still practiced by Family Heirloom Weavers, Red Lion.* **Below:** *Lester P. Breininger, Jr. demonstrates his design techniques.* **Bottom:** *Shards of 18th and 19th century excavated pottery guide master potter Breininger, in crafting his redware.*

LESTER P. BREININGER, JR.

Lester P. Breininger, Jr., has been described as a medieval mystic and a Pennsylvania treasure. One admirer tried to summarize his character as "half alchemist, half folklorist, half genius, and half snake oil salesman."

Breininger laughs heartily at the unmathematical portrait. That fact tells as much about his style, substance, and sense of humor as the dozens of articles on his contributions to Pennsylvania's heritage. A ninth generation Pennsylvania German, Breininger operates a pottery in Robesonia, Berks County, creating folk pottery inspired by 18th and 19th century redware. His work reflects traditional forms and designs brought to this country by the early German-speaking settlers of Pennsylvania. The sgraffito-ware and slipware that come out of his kilns capture a boldness of decoration, creativity, and originality that might seem out of place in a culture focused on survival and practicality.

In the 1960s, when Lester and his wife, Barbara Clay Breininger, purchased a whimsical creation representing a seated dog holding a basket in its mouth, Lester asked a high school faculty colleague, Tom Alexander, to make a "match" for the seated dog.

Alexander said he wouldn't clone a dog "partner," but would show Lester how. So Lester joined an adult art class taught by Alexander, and soon a closely matched pair of seated dogs occupied a place in the Breininger home, followed by a rooster, a duck, and other playful figures to join a menagerie that has not stopped growing.

Copying traditional redware in the Old Country style became an obsession for Lester Breininger. When he became one of eastern Pennsylvania's most ardent preservationists, his enthusiastic spirit swept into homes of friends and neighbors as they helped him and his wife locate samples of redware for study and reproduction.

Lester P. Breininger, Jr., explains how he makes redware in the traditional style

Fragments of pots and figures yielded secrets of early production technologies. From one small shard he could discover how a particular color was achieved. Another showed how a pot was thrown on a wheel or how an accident in the oven resulted in a unique piece.

Speaking of his predecessors in the Pennsylvania German countryside, Breininger explains, "Their palette was rather limited, being mostly yellows, red-browns, greens, and blacks. Actually, clays imported from New Jersey that fired out white appeared yellow under the red lead glaze. However with an array of decorative techniques the redware potters achieved a remarkable range of finished pieces." Colored slips, he continued, could be "trailed, sponged, splotched, combed, feathered, or marbleized to create a variety of effects." Products of the early potteries were generally utilitarian objects such as jugs for vinegar or wine, crocks for sauerkraut, plates and bowls for the table, buttermolds, candlesticks, and pitchers of all shapes and sizes. The items were fragile and easily replaceable, and kept potters occupied in every town and village.

Today, however, collectors dig deep in their pockets to acquire even a modest example of pottery from 18th and 19th century Pennsylvania kilns.

Clay abounds in southeastern Pennsylvania, Breininger writes in his booklet *Potters of the Tulpehocken*. (The Tulpehocken region lies on the western side of Berks County.) He explains, "Whether it be gray, blue, yellow, or red when dug, most local clays turn the characteristic red of earthenware." More rarely the color is red-brown to orange, he says, depending on firing temperatures and mineral content. Iron content is responsible for the red color.

Pennsylvania's woods provided fuel to fire the kilns. A potter required few tools other than a wheel. Glazing materials were acquired from outside the region. "The skill of the potter is of greatest importance in redware production," Breininger writes, and "this process, which seems relatively simple to the onlooker, is amazingly difficult and frustrating to the novice potter."

Most ambitious and remarkable of all the early potters' work, Breininger recounts, is sgraffito. Sgraffito, "to scratch" in Italian, is produced when a vessel is dipped into a colored slip or slip is poured in or on it. Slip is clay with a consistency of cream or gravy. After it is "set up," a sharp tool is used to remove, scratch away, or work off an area, allowing the clay body to show through. Lester's studio shelves reveal a wide variety of creative pieces that delight the eye and the imagination. The artistry of individual potters can be seen in the old and new pieces. The tulip and the distelfink found on many other forms of Pennsylvania German arts and crafts are the most common images found on pottery. A rider on horseback, a smiling dog, or angels floating on air exist as old and new examples.

One potter decorated a jug with a figure possessing a bird's body and a cat's face. This "catbird" is an example of the creativity and "leap of the imagination" that distinguishes the mundane from the exceptional.

As Breininger continues his work as archaeologist, artist, naturalist, historian, writer, and consultant to museums, two talented employees help to keep the Breininger Pottery in the forefront of creative studios. Greg Zieber is the "wheelman" for the shop, and Wesley Muckey is the sgraffito artist and chief decorator. Both are from Berks County and have a keen appreciation for the tradition of local folk crafts. There is no doubt their benefactor and employer has passed on his vision as a potter along with his obsession for authenticity. Their work is inscribed "Breininger Pottery, Robesonia, Pa." and bears the date of creation. Oftimes, in the tradition of the craft, the weather on the day of inscribing is also included on the bottom of a piece with the pottery name and date. The inscription shows pride and foils attempts of unethical persons who would sell the work at the enormous prices being paid on the open market for originals from the heyday of redware making in the region. Special editions of redware sometimes include Greg's or Wes' name, or both, to reflect their contribution in the creation.

Breininger has received many awards, but one prize stands out in his mind: In 1986 the Governor of Pennsylvania awarded him the Hazlett Award for Excellence in the Arts. This recognition puts him in the ranks of Pennsylvania's most influential artists, craftsmen, composers, and performers. His work has been photographed for covers of important magazines and collected by august museums such as the Smithsonian and Winterthur.

For Lester Breininger, the road he travels is short but fruitful. "My people came here in 1712," he states, "and in 250 years we moved west 25 miles."

Left: *Three of these stoneware jugs and crocks with German motifs, collected by Dr. David Bronstein, were made by the Cowden and Wilcox firm of Harrisburg in the mid-1800s.* **Below Left:** *Celtic harp maker, David Drain of Newport, explains his craft at the Little Buffalo Festival of the Arts, Perry County.* **Below:** *At Chimneys, the Boiling Springs luthier school founded and directed by Ed Campbell, a student measures the thickness of the face of a violin with a caliper.* **Bottom:** *Visitors to the Watch and Clock Museum, Columbia, can observe the tools of a clockmaker at this exhibit.*

n the Keystone State, annual festivals that focus on ethnic ties and practices are a highlight of our cultural milieu. Whether secular or religious in nature, these occasions provide a communal experience that builds bonds of friendship.

Those who perform for the attendees of a publicized event are often members of a group that meets regularly throughout the year to hone their skills. Today, participation in an ethnic group can be based on interest as much as lineage. For instance, not all of the musicians in the Klezmer-playing group known as The Old World Folk Band

FOOD, FESTIVALS AND PARADES

Grape stomping,
Renaissance Festival,
Mt. Hope Winery

are Jewish in religion and culture. The Harrisburg–based group, however, values playing authentic music and has heightened its repertoire with songs brought from Russia by a Soviet clarinet player and singer who recently immigrated to Pennsylvania.

The Shooters and Mummers Day Parade in Philadelphia each year has evolved into a world-known phenomenon organized by tightly knit ethnic groups as well as loose associations of neighbors and friends. The yearlong focus of each group is preparing costumes that they hope will please the judges who review this New Year's Day parade.

The ethnic and cultural groups in Pennsylvania that originate in Latin American or southern European regions invite non-member participants to secular events that follow religious services, or they wrap secular activities around the religious focus, inviting spectators to join them before and after the religious observances. An excellent example of this practice lies in Aliquippa, Beaver County, where the San Rocco Festival takes place each August. This festival began about 1925 when citizens who shared origins from Italy decided to honor their patron saint with religious and secular activities. Italian art, music, dance, and food are combined in a week-long offering that includes a grand fireworks display by the famous Zambelli company.

*Costumes,
Mummers Parade,
Philadelphia*

Special guests like the Bishop of Pittsburgh are honored, too, along with the older members of the Italian community who have made outstanding contributions to the festival and the traditions being passed to younger generations. The festival culminates on Sunday when a group of selected individuals present the San Rocco Banner early in the morning. The San Rocco Mass is held at St. Titus Catholic Church, followed by a procession in which a sculpture of the saint is carried through the streets in a neighborhood called Sheffield Terrace.

Throughout the festival, community residents and hundreds of visitors can learn an Italian folk dance, the *tarantella*, and watch craftsmen make bobbin lace. Children and adults not familiar with *chiambelli*, the special loaves of bread used in the festival, can learn how to make this culinary delight, and they can immerse themselves in music from Italian opera to Italian folk songs.

The San Rocco Festival is only one Pennsylvania event that has grown from a one- or two-day celebration to an occasion stretching for a week or longer.

The Italians of Pennsylvania are among the many citizens who hold special events to mark Columbus Day, and the entire population of the state is invited to honor William Penn and the founding of Pennsylvania. Most notable of these annual events are the ones in Ambridge, Beaver County; Titusville, Crawford County; Horsham, Montgomery County; and Northumberland, Northumberland County. Volunteerism, one of Pennsylvanian's greatest resources, organizes these festivities that promote outpourings of respect, rejoicing, or high revelry.

Oddly enough, some groups create observances that might seem contradictory to tradition, such as the Quakers do when local meetinghouses become known for their Christmas Eve services. A Quaker spokesman passing on traditions of the Society of Friends points out that early Quakers believed that every day was holy and that observing Christmas day in a special way was not necessary or desirable.

The origin of community celebrations has been lost in the mists of time. But many folklorists believe that festivals, parades, and feasts first came about because of the anxieties of early people who did not understand the forces of nature and wished to placate them. Since most ancient festivals and feasts were associated with planting and harvest times, or with honoring the dead, it is not surprising that they have continued as secular festivals, with some religious overtones, into modern times.

Pennsylvania's Mexican population, for example, follows home country tradition when they hold feasts around the graves and tombs of departed family member on November 2, *El dia de Los Muertos* or "Day of the Dead." Participants make offerings of flowers, earthen pots of food, toys, and gifts, along with the burning of candles and incense.

The timing of seasonal festivals is determined by the solar and lunar calendars and by the cycle of the seasons. Pennsylvania's Asian people, especially in the larger communities found in Pittsburgh and Philadelphia, join their relatives in the homeland by celebrating the Chinese New Year for an entire month in late January or February with gaiety, parades, and theatrical performances.

Historical customs are perpetuated in these seasonal festivals, too. An example is Homstrom, celebrated on February 3 by those of Swiss ancestry. This event exults in the end of winter with the burning of straw people representing Old Man Winter. Pennsylvania's quirky Groundhog Day, observed on February 2 each year, also is tied to end-of-winter mythology.

The most famous of seasonal festivities, set by the church calendar but secular in tone, are the pre-Lenten carnivals of European and Latin American peoples climaxing with the many Mardi Gras, or Fat Tuesday, festivities. Pennsylvania has put its own special touch on this seasonal occasion with its annual Fasnacht Day, brought to life by the early Pennsylvania Germans. Following age-old religious practices, the cooks of the

Pennsylvania German household used all the fat available in the home and fried special doughnut-like cakes called *fasnachts*. This practice removed some of the temptations that might be faced by those in the household sacrificing heavy foods for the Lenten observance.

The enjoyment of Fasnacht Day in Pennsylvania is no longer limited to the "Pennsylvania Dutch," and we are as likely to find groups of Italian or Irish descent making "fasnachts" to sell as a fund-raiser as historical groups tracing lineage to the early Pennsylvania Germans.

Ancestral traditions are poignantly expressed in harvest feasts, festivals, and parades in every corner of Pennsylvania. The York Fair in York County is a solid example, dating from the days of the Penn family, of Pennsylvania communities staging expositions to celebrate the year's harvests. The state's Department of Agriculture promotes fairs extensively throughout Pennsylvania, and among the dozens of annual events are 20 major fairs spread throughout the rectangular region named for the founder.

Some fairs are more than just expositions of the biggest pumpkin and the biggest sunflower. They are held to produce income for nonprofit causes. For instance, the Big Brothers/Big Sisters Fair in Meadow Lands, Washington County, begins the fair season in June and benefits local children.

Garden produce, York County Fair

A little later in the season the United Way of Columbia County Fair takes place in Bloomsburg, Columbia County, and then comes the Meadville Sertoma Club Fair in Crawford County. Also unfolding in the early days of summer are the Big Butler Fair in Butler County, the Dayton Horsemen Fair in Armstrong County, and the Gratz Area Antique Machinery Association Days in Dauphin County. County fairs in Lycoming, Clearfield, Wayne, Greene, Washington, Erie, Crawford, Indiana, Juniata, Armstrong, Mercer, and Columbia add to a season rich in agricultural diversity and ethnic expression in art, dance, food, music, and customs.

Visitors to these fairs and the people who operate them enjoy a variety of ethnic foods. Church groups, civic clubs, and family businesses, to name a few, are among the groups that make these colorful affairs occasions to remember. Children who attend these festivities may get their first taste of a Greek gyro, a Pennsylvania Dutch funnel cake, a Chinese egg roll, an Italian cheese steak, a Polish sausage, or Native American frybread. Many groups promote ethnic events happening within their churches or clubs while selling ethnic food and raising funds to enhance programming, add buildings, or conduct classes and services tied to Old World traditions.

Festivities, whatever their make-up, provide an opportunity for adults to pass on folk knowledge and the meaning of family stories to younger generations and enrich the understanding of their heritage. At the same time, they transcend personal concerns and unite citizens into a cooperative spirit that benefits everyone.

Cooperation among all peoples and the blessings enjoyed by them are centered in the official and unofficial observances of Thanksgiving in Pennsylvania. One of the important events leading to the establishment of the Thanksgiving holiday in the United States took place in Pennsylvania, when Congress declared a day of national thanksgiving following the American victory at Brandywine.

Just as popular as the harvest festivals that offer ethnic populations an opportunity to participate and carry on traditions are the festivals that focus on a particular crop. But grape festivals begun by immigrants from France and apple festivals originating in Quaker orchards have been supplanted by festivals bringing all cultures together for the enjoyment of foods that seem to grow and taste better in Pennsylvania. Among these are strawberries, rhubarb, cherries, peaches and, yes, mushrooms.

Festivals can have important significance related to national identity such as the victory festival, the *Cinco de Mayo*, Mexico's commemoration of its defeat of the French at the Battle of Puebla on May 5, 1862. This festival is observed not only in Mexico, Los

Christmas traditions in York County home

Angeles, and other U.S. cities with large Mexican-American populations, but also in many towns and cities in Pennsylvania.

Most Pennsylvania ethnic groups celebrate special occasions observed in their homelands from Bastille Day for the French in Pennsylvania to the Gandhi Jayanti, a festival held in India on the birthday (October 2) of Mohandas K. ("Mahatma") Gandhi. The Finns hold parades and ceremonies dedicated to the Finnish national epic, the Kalevala, and its 19th century editor, the scholar Elias Lönnrot, and the Welsh of Pennsylvania recreate their edition of the most famous festival in Wales, the Royal National Eisteddfod, held in August to honor the finest talent in Welsh literature and music.

Some Austrian groups in Pennsylvania hold cultural events to coincide with the annual Salzburg Festival of Music, and Germans from Berks to Lawrence counties recreate Octoberfest in some form or fashion. One of the most festive days in the Pennsylvania calendar is St. Patrick's Day, when it is said everyone in the pub, the tavern, the county, and the state becomes Irish for the day.

Despite raw March weather, celebrations usually begin with a parade. Two of the state's finest bring large crowds of onlookers to Scranton and Pittsburgh. Among school marching bands and floats built by fraternal organizations are Irish dance groups and pipe bands.

Pennsylvania has ties to a relatively recent holiday festival in which arts, lore, and customs of various regions of Africa are merged into the cultural festival known as Kwanzaa. From the Swahili word *kwanza* for "beginnings," Kwanzaa was created with the help of Maulana Karenga, born Ron Everett, who lived for a year in Pennsylvania and was graduated in 1958 from William Penn High School in York. Karenga eventually became a professor and chairman of black studies at California State University in Long Beach.

The festival is celebrated with special meals, stories, and songs in the home for seven days and nights from December 26 to January 1. The African colors of green, black, and red are displayed, and the adults lead discussions and readings that emphasize five fundamental values:

    1. Unity of family, friends, and community;

    2. Reverence for the creator and creation, which encompasses an appreciation of, and respect for, the environment;

    3. Commemoration of the past, which includes honoring one's ancestors and valuing one's heritage;

    4. Commitment to the cultural ideals of the African community, which include truth, justice, and mutual respect; and

    5. A celebration of the "Good of Life" and appreciation for the blessings of achievement, family, and community.

Other festivals of ethnic origin crowd the calendar with outpourings of dance, art, film, and theater springing from the traditions of the many nations represented in Pennsylvania. One such festival or, in this case, Pow Wow, takes place in Sullivan County. At Forksville, where the Big and Little Loyalsock creeks meet, the Eastern Delaware Nations Pow Wow takes place every year in June.

This annual event began in Philadelphia and moved to the Sullivan County Fairgrounds in the mid-1980s. Typically, 200 dancers assemble near a roped-off circle. Drummers and singers provide a rhythmic and reverent backdrop as dancers follow a leader carrying the Delaware Nations staff into the circle. The staff has a circle on top of it and is adorned with feathers. A staff, flag, or banner from each nation represented can be seen as the line of dancers snakes around a fire burning in the center of the circle. The American flag is also in evidence and everyone is invited to celebrate the unity being represented on the grounds surrounded by steep, lush hills and gurgling waters.

Among the dancers here are natives from Canada, Mexico, South America, the Dominican Republic, and Puerto Rico, as well as many of the states in the USA. During the gathering, officially scheduled for three days, but extended by many participants who arrive early and stay late, the mood is much like that of a family reunion. Individuals have time to see old friends and make new ones. The philosophical have time to compare notes with other like-minded people, and children who just want to have fun can engage in activities that nurture their spirits as well as their bodies. Vendors are on hand to provide Indian tacos, Indian fry bread, buffalo burgers, Mohawk corn soup, pork and white beans, barbecued chicken and, yes, even funnel cake, that inimitable Pennsylvania favorite usually associated with the southeastern tier of the state. Individuals and groups set up stands where they offer leather goods, boots, moccasins, jewelry, literature and many other wares. Prices range from a couple nickels to a couple hundred dollars.

In a recent edition of this annual event, one of the honored guests was Chief Standing Bear, a resident of Norwich, Connecticut, from the Mohican nation. Chief Standing Bear attends about 50 Native American occasions each year with his wife, Cindy Rose Moon, and their children. Sitting under a canopy that faced the circle of dance, Chief Standing Bear offered a visitor his views of this festival, of Native American unity, and of tradition. He observed that Indians and others need to protect each other's rights so that no people will be oppressed. "We can learn a great lesson from the smallest creatures on earth," he said. Perhaps he meant the ant or the beaver. "When we work together, we can move mountains."

The festivals of many ethnic and national groups are credited with the preservation of unique customs, folktales, costumes, and culinary skills. In Pennsylvania there is a sharing of cultures that is rare in many other states and regions and the richness of Pennsylvania traditions is sometimes surprising even to residents born and reared here. Even the tradition of the Christmas tree, celebrated by so many people in America, is said to have Pennsylvania origins, and an old mythical character brought here by the early Pennsylvania Germans, the Belsnickel, is said to have evolved into the modern day Santa Claus. And mentioning one more addition to Pennsylvania's cache of cultural contributions will point to the fact that there is so much more to be discovered when exploring the state's influence on America and the global community.

A folk artist in Berks County, Johannes Bolich, may have put onto paper the first image ever seen of the Easter Bunny. A colored drawing dated before 1811 portrays a rabbit carrying eggs in a basket harnessed to his back. The eggs are decorated and, according to one well-known history professor, this may be the oldest representation of the Easter Rabbit in American folk life.

As communities and society grow and change, the characteristics of their traditional festivals and feasts grow and change, too.

This overview of Pennsylvania festivals and parades gives but a small taste of how people bring old traditions to the state and allow them to alter or decline, while elsewhere new ones emerge. A roll call of all the festivals, parades, and feasts in Pennsylvania would be impressive, but a unifying theme rings clear. In all these events the vitality and exuberance of Pennsylvania are blended with respect for the earth and the traditional ways of ancestors.

Previous Page: *The Scotch-Irish and others who love the heritage attend the Ligonier Highland Games to enjoy competitions. A Scottish athlete pitches a 20-pound sheaf of hay in a burlap sack over a bar that is raised by six-inch intervals.* **Below:** *The Loch Rannoch and Bucks Caledonian pipe bands play at the Scottish Heritage Festival at Graeme Park, Horsham.* **Right:** *In Highland dress, as required, a competitor tries for a prize in the 22-pound hammer throw at the Ligonier games.* **Below Right:** *A Celtic harp concert entertains visitors at the Westmoreland County festival.*

Previous Pages: *Scranton's St. Patrick's Day parade stirs ethnic pride among the Irish* et al. **Below:** *Displaying whatever praises the Irish and their country goes at Pittsburgh's St. Patrick's Day festivities.* **Right:** *Sporting Irish green, Pittsburghers flock downtown to watch the city's annual St. Patrick's Day parade.* **Next Pages:** *York has made its Halloween Parade a yearly Sunday afternoon event that features costumed community organizations. Families stake out a viewing spot along the sidewalk hours in advance.*

BETTY GROFF

Cooking from the heart and soul is as natural to Betty Groff as the watercress growing in the creek behind her house. Praised by thousands of guests who have sampled her Pennsylvania Dutch hospitality, she remains modest. News anchor Tom Brokaw is one of her most ardent fans, and in her storage room she proudly displays a bed where James Beard, the rotund chef, once slept with aromas of Betty's culinary art wafting through the early-morning air.

Betty, a descendant of Hans Herr, a pioneer leader of the region, grew up on the family farm in Lancaster County. The Herr family was famous for smoked meats and Persian melons. Betty's grandmother experimented with hybridizing vegetables and produced a melon that attracted the Burpee Company to the family farm early in the 1900s. Partly because her Mennonite upbringing taught her to shun personal aggrandizement, she turned down offers to sell rights to a new, improved melon, or to air her life story on national radio. Betty's grandmother and grandfather tutored the young protégé in food preparation and economics of farm life.

When Betty married Abe Groff, a young man from another Lancaster farm, a food dynasty was established. "Abe's family operated a dairy farm," Betty said, "so we had the best of both worlds for use in our kitchens."

"We lived a simple life," Betty says of her Mennonite upbringing, "but when we all sat down at a special meal, extravagance was always on the table." The Mennonites, one of several sects of "Plain People" in Pennsylvania, share values of hard work and thrift with the Brethren, Dunkards, Amish, Schwenkfelders, and other groups known for their devotion to the Creator in everyday life as well as their down-to-earth lifestyle.

Early in her marriage to Abe Groff, Betty's zest for life led her to invite strangers into her home, where she would prepare authentic Pennsylvania Dutch dinners and serve them as her family had for many generations. When Betty and Abe served family-style meals, the abundance from the field and the imagination of the cook led to memorable experiences. As providing meals for guests filled the family home to overflowing, the couple bought the old Simon Cameron summer mansion to cater elegant events such as weddings and anniversary parties. Cameron, President Lincoln's first secretary of war, installed aerated fishponds on the property and brought in trout and other varieties of fish the Groffs still use today.

A typical meal for the Groffs, precisely emulated in their restaurant, occurs at tables set with starched damask and polished silver. The fare depends on the season. In summer, fresh produce from gardens and markets dictates menu direction. In winter, the contents of the cold cellar or freezers guide the chef. Whatever the season, though, smoked meats from the butcher's best stock are included. After the family observes a quiet prayer, Betty passes a plate piled high with squares of chocolate or coconut cake. "Dessert is too good to save until last," Betty believes. "So let's have a little sweet before we spoil our appetites." The hostess passes bowls, plates, and platters heaped with steaming entrees and tempting side dishes. A rectangular bowl of chow chow, a blend of colorful pickled vegetables; an oval bowl of *smiercase*, a kind of cottage cheese, followed by apple butter, an unusual combination for most visitors, but too good to pass by. A round platter of carved turkey is

An expert in
Pennsylvania
Dutch cuisine,
Betty Groff
shows how
to roll out
potpie noodles.

followed by a bowl of *schnitz und knepp*, dried apples cooked slowly with fat dumplings and lumps of smoked ham. A plate of baked sausage, seasoned with a secret Groff combination of herbs and spices, is followed by apple sauce, cole slaw made with cabbage squeezed by hand, mashed potatoes, and red beet eggs. Special vegetables and greens: dandelion leaves with bacon drippings, creamed spinach, sugar peas drowned in sweet butter, green beans with mushrooms, baby carrots, sun-ripened tomatoes, and corn pudding, define the season.

A pitcher of gravy is passed, a bowl of freshly ground horseradish, especially good with the sausage, and then a big plate of filling, sometimes with almonds or pecans, sometimes with raisins or oysters.

Certain times of the year dishes featuring wild game—pheasant, grouse, rabbit, squirrel—and local fish—shad, trout, bass, or catfish—tempt palates. Clams, mussels, and Chesapeake crabs may find their way to the table, too, depending on the season and the menu planner's whims.

And a traditional hog maw, a pig's stomach stuffed with potatoes, sausage, celery, carrots, onion, and herbs, would not be out of place here, nor would a stuffed goose or a roast duck with maple-ginger sauce and wild rice.

No sooner does the parade of plates, bowls and platters end, than it begins again. Dishes reappear and make another round. But it seems the meal has hardly begun when it's time to pass dessert. Shoofly pie, anyone? *Schnitz* pie? Blueberry crumb pie? Montgomery pie? Strawberry rhubarb crumble or black walnut cake? What is your pleasure? A tiny sliver of each, perhaps.

Over the decades that have passed since Betty and Abe began their venture into Pennsylvania Dutch hospitality, they have sold the Cameron home and given each of their children parcels of land to build their own homes. Betty and Abe now live in a home at the corner of the farm across the street from the original farmhouse where the restaurant still serves Betty's home-style dinners and the chef's à la carte features. Along the way, they have transformed the farm property into a picture-perfect golf resort. The natural springs and rolling meadows of the golf course provide a unique experience.

Today, Betty and Abe operate a personalized Bed and Breakfast in their spacious home across the road from Groff's Farm Restaurant and Golf Club. Betty is the author of several best-selling cookbooks and continues to write "from the heart and soul" about cooking and the family traditions that nurture her zest for life. A television cooking show and coverage in national and international media have allowed her to pass on the traditions of the Pennsylvania Germans to people around the world. She still invites the entire family for a festive dinner at her own table.

From her made-for-cameras modern kitchen in Mount Joy, Lancaster County, to New York City, and media appearances around the world, Betty Groff continues to pass on Pennsylvania traditions she loves—with plenty of food, plenty of stories, and plenty of laughs to go around.

Below: *Mexican chicken burrito, beef taco, and cheese enchilada (center) are menu items at Lupita's Mexican Restaurant that are served with Mexican rice and fried beans. Carne azada (grilled steak) is served here with green onion, melted cheese with corizso, green salad, frijoles de la olla (pinto beans) and fresh guacamole and tortillas.* **Right:** *Dishes from central Pennsylvania's Thai Bangkok Wok Restaurant are (clockwise) jasmine Rice; shrimp pad Thai, a peanut-topped rice noodle dish; Thai rolls with pineapple sauce; Tum Yum Talay, seafood soup with lemon grass; and smoked chili sauce.*

Left: *This Pennsylvania German menu features (clock-wise) coleslaw, chicken potpie, and strawberry shortcake.* **Below Left:** *Middle Eastern foods from Shab's Pita Stroller, Harrisburg, include (clockwise) squares of baklava, a sweet pastry; tabouli, a cracked wheat salad with feta cheese; stuffed grape leaves; baba ghannouj, eggplant spread; and hommous, a chick pea spread.*
Below: *Harrisburg's Passage To India offers (clockwise) vegetable soup with vegetables and lentils seasoned with mustard seeds, cumin, and fennel seeds; tandoori chicken, marinated in yogurt, ginger, garlic, lemon juice and fresh spices; zucchini masala; and vegetable fritters.*

Above: From the kitchen of Shenandoah resident Jean Kiskeravage, who is second generation Polish, kiski, babka and perogies on the right are all made from potatoes. On the blue plate kabusta (sauerkraut), smoked and fresh kielbasa are shown with kotleti (meatballs) (center) and ksian (horseradish). A Polish brandy is also served. **Right:** The Polish dessert kolacki, also made by Jean, is a rolled cookie with nuts.

125

Right: *Embroidery is featured at a Pittsburgh Folk Festival booth for Slovakia.* **Bottom Right:** *Festivals provide artisans and vendors a place to market handcrafted items, food, and keepsakes that remind one of the home country.* **Below:** *Booths that sell authentic ethnic foods are popular at festivals, here at the Pittsburgh Folk Festival.* **Next Pages:** *A procession through Sheffield Terrace, a neighborhood within Aliquippa, culminates the San Rocco Festival, which honors the Italian heritage of these Beaver County residents.*

Above: *Descendants of Italian immigrants carry their family banners during the San Rocco Festival, a Pennsylvania event named after the patron saint of Patrica, Italy.* **Right:** *White-robed men of St. Titus Catholic parish carry a statue of San Rocco after the Sunday morning mass. Sixteen chiambellis, golden brown doughnut-shaped biscuits, adorn each foot of the statue, one for each man carrying. August 16 is the patron saint's day.*

Below: *Held annually in June, the Delaware Nations Pow-Wow of Sullivan County provides opportunity for Native American groups from many areas of the United States and several other countries to meet, learn, and enjoy dances. A dramatic part of the festival is the Grand Entry when all nations come together in a dance.* **Right:** *Native attire adorned in furs, shells, leather, and feathers is worn at the festival held at Indian Steps Museum, York County.*

Above Left: *Demonstrations of Old World skills at festivals give onlookers an appreciation of craftsmanship brought to early America. Darryl Yeager of Bellwood turns a piece on a lathe for one of his handmade wooden toys.* **Left:** *Magic tricks such as fire-eating provide entertainment at ethnic festivals.* **Above:** *A Native American descendent displays a headdress at the Indian Steps festival in York County.* **Top:** *Marie L. Tallman explains quiltmaking at the Kutztown Pennsylvania German Festival.*

chapter five

Individuals, families, and many kinds of associations are collaborating in Pennsylvania to keep ethnic traditions alive. By visiting landmarks and historic places where Old World artisans ply their trades, people walk in the steps of those who came before them. By participating in feasts, festivals, and parades, they learn skills, use art forms, and absorb culture that makes them feel connected, distinct, or privileged.

The distinctive patterns and practices inherent in these efforts are as diverse as the people who produce them. Each group reveals its secrets to the next generation in personal and public activities. In

KEEPING TRADITIONS ALIVE

Latifah Shabazz promotes African-American heritage at her Harrisburg shop, "Creative Expressions"

most cases, these viewpoints or understandings are shared with the larger community in forms ranging from evangelistic fervor to reverent goodwill.

A Greek Orthodox Church teaches its youth the language and dances, while a mosque inculcates its children with Koranic wisdom in English as well as Arabic. Families set aside areas of their homes or their backyards for tributes to saints or ancestors, and some burn candles and use musical instruments to express ideals rooted in the past. The fashions in which these ideals are nurtured and passed on are as diverse as the individuals and the groups who assume the role of teacher, guardian, shaman, or pathfinder.

One of the many individuals in Pennsylvania who infuse the spirit of goodwill through all the ethnic, religious, and cultural groups they encounter is Latifah Shabazz of Dauphin County. While some benefactors use a pulpit or a parade ground to carry on their mission, Latifah works out of an African shop in the Capital City's midtown district. Selling handmade crafts fashioned by neighbors in Harrisburg and by contacts throughout the African continent, she also promotes unity, pride, personal integrity, and peace of mind. Latifah is the daughter of the late Walter and Jean Acey, Methodists who made their home in Harrisburg's Uptown district. The couple raised their two daughters, Latifah, born Verne, and Towanda, to respect everybody and to view the world not only from their inner-city neighborhood, but also from places they visited and the places their elders visited. Latifah heard stories about slavery, sharecropping, and how people triumphed over hardship. Her father was stationed in North Africa during World War II. He shared many stories of military service and related how he was able to build a future with support and encouragement from God and friends and family back home.

Latifah's grandmother, Sarah Jones, was a civil rights worker before the title entered the American vocabulary. With a deep-rooted village perception, she worked for the rights of seniors, lobbying community and government leaders for the rights of older Pennsylvanians. She formed an organization later called the Uptown Senior Center that is still in operation today. Latifah's mother had inherited the social activist traits of her parents and when the time was right the same traits were passed on to Latifah and her sister.

During the 1970s, as the United States was experiencing a resurgence of African-American pride, Latifah was recruited by a college in New Hampshire.

"This was the era of Afro hairstyles and buttons that proclaimed, 'I'm Black and I'm Proud,'" Latifah remembers. "And I wore my button to classes without any apology. My classmates and professors knew where I stood." Soon the culture shock she experienced at attending a college in New England dissolved.

When the college closed she was saddened, but she faced new challenges on the campus where she resumed her education, this time in West Virginia. An Islamic mosque was located near the college town and it was in that mosque that Latifah found another path to her spiritual development. She became a Muslim, changed her name, and through the years has reconciled her early religious teachings with a worldwide vision that includes explorations along other spiritual paths. "Today I feel quite content," she says, summarizing her spiritual journey. "I am free in the understanding that many religions reflect the power of God in the universe. I feel that Inner Light that seems to be present in the beliefs of people all over the world."

Latifah's world is full of color, vibrancy, and diversity. Her shop on North Third Street exudes an atmosphere that reflects the African marketplace. An impromptu poetry reading is as welcome here as a recital from a three-year old who is eager, or not so eager, to sing a new song that she has learned. A customer from Asia stops by to retrieve a supply of herbs from the room where Latifah serves tea, and a community leader drops off a collection of art for an exhibition Latifah is organizing.

Among the things for sale are drawings and jewelry Latifah creates and handmade crafts that vendors from Africa have left at her store on consignment. High above the shelves in her shop are tribal masks, small rugs, and other objects from Africa. The shelves are lined with carvings, special soaps, and incense.

There are items used in the Kwanzaa holiday: the *kinara*, the candleholder representing a stalk of corn from which the family grows; the *mishumaa*, seven candles (3 red, 3 green, 1 black) standing for Kwanzaa's seven principles; the *mkeka*, a straw placemat, recalling tradition and history; the *mazao*, a variety of fruit, symbolizing the harvest; the *vibunzi*, an ear of corn for each child, celebrating the child's potential; the *kikombe cha umoja*, a cup of unity, commemorating one's ancestors, and *zawadi*, modest gifts, encouraging creativity, achievement, and success.

The shop carries clothing like dashikis from Nigeria, capstans from Ghana, and hand-woven scarves from Guatemala.

"I feel truly blessed," Latifah offers. "For years I struggled to be a social worker in the tradition of my family upbringing. I have found a way to fulfill that mission at the same time I am building a business. And the business not only helps me but the people around me. It gives people of African heritage a place, much like they would find in an African village, to see African art and wares. Most importantly, it's a place where people of all traditions can meet and greet each other in a welcoming atmosphere that nurtures understanding and a connection to the Motherland."

In Pennsylvania, the diversity in ethnic, religious, and cultural groups is nurtured by numerous organizations established to demonstrate how cooperation benefits and enriches the landscape as a whole. The Balch Institute located in Philadelphia and the Institute for Cultural Partnerships headquartered in Harrisburg are two institutions that work to maximize the cooperation and understanding among diverse groups.

Representing more than 80 ethnic groups, the Balch Institute preserves multicultural awareness and documents and interprets the ethnic and immigrant experience in the broader tapestry of the United States. A non-profit organization, the Balch Institute operates a museum and library on South Seventh Street. Building a base of knowledge focused on new immigrant groups and involving communities, schools, and individuals in educational and cultural programs, the Balch invites visitors to on- and off-site programs. The institute has formed partnerships with several organizations housed there including Temple University's Center for Immigration Research, the Philadelphia Jewish Archives Center, and the Free Library of Philadelphia Independence Branch. Drawing on its collection of more than 5,000 objects, 65,000 volumes, 6,000 serial titles, 6,000 reels of microfilm, and 20,000 photographs, the Balch has played a large role in demonstrating interdependence of global communities.

Dr. Shalom Staub at his Harrisburg office

A like-minded organization that complements the Balch is the Institute for Cultural Partnerships in Harrisburg. The Institute strives to "help individuals and communities to live, learn, and work successfully in an increasingly diverse society." ICP staff members include president and CEO Shalom Staub, Ph.D. In 1987, the governor of Pennsylvania appointed Staub to be the Executive Director of the Pennsylvania Heritage Affairs Commission. In that capacity he worked with leaders in 50 ethnic communities. Addressing "everyday issues" of cultural diversity, the ICP "works with large corporations, small businesses, health care providers, social service agencies, local governments, and schools and universities to meet the challenges and take advantage of the opportunities offered by our diverse society."

"Our communities and workplaces increasingly reflect ethnic, racial, gender, language, disability, sexual orientation, age, and religious diversity," Dr. Staub believes. "And these demographic changes affect all levels of organizational structures and business interactions." Other organizations throughout Pennsylvania support specific ethnic groups in specific ways. In the late 1800s and early 1900s, a number of "fraternal" organizations were established to help immigrants feel more comfortable in their adopted country while preserving aspects of their homeland. The Slovene National Benefit Society based in Enon Valley, Lawrence County, and the Serb National Federation, based in Pittsburgh, are two such associations. These organizations began to offer affordable life insurance policies to members of their ethnic community. They also helped preserve the heritage, culture, traditions, history, and music of the group they served. The Slovene National Benefit Society, for instance, operates a Slovenian Heritage Center that takes visitors on a journey to the Old World, showcasing authentic Slovenian costumes, household items, artwork, and crafts.

Change is a constant in global affairs and fraternal organizations that serve ethnic groups, and one association that has adapted to change in many ways is the Orthodox Society of America. George G. Lichvarik, president of OSA since 1982, reflects on the conditions in Eastern Europe from about 1885 to about 1940 as he recounts the history of his association.

"When you throw rocks into the water they cause ripples," he observes. "The conflicts in Eastern Europe spread out over the surface of the continent. My ancestors were Orthodox Russians living along the Carpatho Mountains, and they decided to seek opportunity in America like people living in the nations that surrounded Russia." Lichvarik recounts that many of the early settlers in America went to work in high-risk jobs like the

A child learns from a potter at the Goshenhoppen Festival, Montgomery County

Nutritionist Grace Lefever, York County, promoter of wholistic health traditions

coal mines and the railroads. Insurance companies were reluctant to write polices so the leaders of various ethnic groups formed companies of their own. "The welfare of wives and children was uppermost in their minds," Lichvarik says. Formation of these ethnic associations helped to unite communities and to perpetuate the traditions of the old countries.

The OSA was founded in Monessen, Westmoreland County, in 1915, and originally was called the United Russian Orthodox Association. Lichvarik reports that soon the association moved its offices to Pittsburgh and operated there for many decades. Leaders moved headquarters to North Olmstead, Ohio, in 1997 to reflect the geographic shift of its 4,000 members. Today the organization serves all orthodox Christians. Like most volunteers and paid staff in organizations that serve ethnic groups, George Lichvarik inherited his role from his parents, who were active in the early days of the OSA operations. Lichvarik also serves as editor of the OSA Messenger, a bi-monthly publication that addresses lodge, church, and social events as well as newsworthy happenings affecting its members in Pennsylvania, New Jersey, Ohio, Michigan, Indiana, Illinois, and West Virginia.

Transcending cultural differences but preserving traditions that unite and enrich, people like Latifah Shabazz and George Lichvarik, working in broad urban areas, have counterparts in rural Pennsylvania. Grace Lefever, in the tradition of her Church of the Brethren upbringing, has been widely recognized for her efforts to surpass differences and preserve traditions to the benefit of all. From Stoverstown, York County, she is passing on traditions learned from the people of her religious denomination, from the Native Americans, from European sources, and from people arriving more recently in Pennsylvania.

Grace lives on a unique homestead that has become a productive farm and a center for the practice and teaching of holistic living. The farm has spurred the development of a health food supermarket and sponsors programs promoting dialogue on issues of healthy living, the environment, and other social issues.

In 1955 Grace married Tim Lefever, a widower with three children. Tim, a descendent of French Huguenots and a member of the Church of the Brethren, was a proponent of organic farming and began to share his thoughts and knowledge of natural food production with Grace, who discovered two little books, *Herbs and the Fountain of Youth* and *Nature's Healing Grasses*.

She read voraciously on the subject and was especially impressed with the knowledge the Native Americans had of the earth and its plants. When Tim and Grace married she moved to has a well-chosen site in southern York County and Grace's life changed direction. She began selling fresh-ground flour and produce from their gardens to friends. Demand soon exceeded supply. With a friend, Paul Keene, Tim founded the Pennsylvania chapter of the Natural Food Associates. This group later changed its named to the Pennsylvania Natural Living Association. The Lefever property, enjoying southern exposure and fertile land, took on some of the attributes of a college campus and some aspects of a crop-testing homestead. The farm is called Sonnewald, Pennsylvania German for "sunny woods." Stewards of this 60-acre plot have ensured that no unnatural fertilizers have been used on this land for more than 40 years.

After Tim died in 1986, his daughter Willa moved to Pennsylvania to help operate the business that had grown around healthy eating and to pass on the traditions rooted in religious, cultural, and ethnic pride—all leading folks to eat better and live healthier, happier lives. Willa and Grace have perpetuated Tim Lefever's vision and expanded it.

"Underneath our skin," Grace says with a light in her eye, "all people are made of the same physical and spiritual fabric. Keeping the body healthy is a key to keeping our families, communities, and nations healthy in body, mind, and spirit."

Below: *Three generations of the Kapeluck Family do pysanky, Ukrainian egg decorating, in their home before Easter.*
Right: *Michael Kapeluck's steady hand guides a kistka or writing tool to apply a design with beeswax on an uncooked egg before beginning the dyeing process.*

JOANNE STAROSCHAK

Joanne Staroschak has never questioned her mission as a teacher. For more than 50 years she has shared the art, crafts, and culture of her native Ukraine with her Pennsylvania neighbors. Thousands have learned "pysanky," the ancient art of egg dyeing, thanks to Staroschak's enchantment with her heritage. Her work reflects family stories and episodes from the history of her homeland. The beautiful eggs illustrate the exploits of Kyiv and his brothers, Shchek and Khorev, and their sister, Lybed. Together they founded the city of Kyiv, sometimes spelled Kiev, the capital city of Ukraine, hundreds of years before the birth of Christ.

Kyiv was the prince of the Slavic tribe inhabiting the region and the capital city named for him is located in North Central Ukraine on the Dnipro River, which flows to the Black Sea. Strategically located on both East-West and North-South trading routes, Kyiv became the largest city in Ukraine, with a population of 2,600,000 people.

Ukrainians have found many unique ways to pass along their culture. In addition to pysanky, songs are also used as culture bearers. One type of song, the duma, recounts battles, laments, occupations, and escapes experienced by Ukrainians in the 16th and 17th centuries. Kobzars, blind musicians, strolled the countryside singing and plucking their banduras, stringed Ukrainian instruments resembling a harpsichord.

Joanne was teaching these cherished traditions to children in her kindergarten classes in the 1940s when war tore apart the region where she was born. In Germany, she met a United States serviceman, a first-generation Ukrainian, who would one day become her husband.

She immigrated to the United States in 1948 and soon was reunited with the serviceman she had met in Germany. She married Metro Staroschak in 1949.

Metro's parents had left Ukraine around the turn of the century and eventually settled in McKees Rocks, Allegheny County, where other immigrants from their homeland were finding jobs as coal miners, railroaders, factory hands, and millworkers. Metro was born here and the young couple chose to make this town their home after they were married. In the past 50 years Joanne has filled their home with the art and crafts of Ukraine.

Inspired by a love of her heritage, a creative mind, and skillful hands, she became a master at the art of "pysanky," also known as "egg-writing." Pysanky is one of the customs associated with the Easter holiday throughout eastern Europe and many regions in this great land have developed distinguishable types of designs recognizable to the learned eye. Like many such customs, it was a pre-Christian practice into which Christian symbolism was later introduced. Some of the motifs reflect the idea of the springtime reawakening of the natural world after winter dormancy. Flowers like the periwinkle and farmyard creatures like the chicken can be suggested in

Joanne Staroschak has taught thousands about Ukranian traditions.

designs, as well as the cross, representing the resurrection of Christ, and the triangle, symbolizing the Trinity. Some eggs feature complex geometric patterns and colors are always important for their symbolic qualities.

Decorated eggs traditionally were given as gifts and sometimes placed at key points in the home, barn, or field to bring prosperity for the coming year. In some homes families set aside a special area where they display eggs that have been received as gifts along with family photographs, carvings from Ukraine, and religious items such as images of saints, palm leaves, and pussy willow branches.

The practice of pysanky integrates religion, ethnicity, and artistic expression. It helps communities to maintain their identity as Ukrainians among themselves and to outsiders. In pysanky, white eggs are decorated using water dyes, beeswax, candles, and a copper-tipped stylus. The copper stylus is heated in the flame of a lighted candle, and then placed on the beeswax to melt a droplet or two into the cone of the stylus. The melted beeswax is applied in fine lines onto the egg, creating intricate designs recognized for their symmetrical patterns. Joanne creates works of striking originality using typical symbols such as the flower petal, chevrons, and multi-colored checkerboards. With each step in the process completed, the work of art becomes more complex and more beautiful.

The first layer of beeswax applied to the egg covers the areas the artist wishes to remain white in the finished design. The artist then dips the egg into the lightest color dye. Subsequently she dips the egg into darker shades of dyes, using black, red, blue, and other colors. Some examples contain seven or more colors. The process is repeated with the beeswax covering areas of the design to be preserved in each particular color. Finally, all the beeswax is melted off the egg to reveal the finished design.

Joanne prefers to use raw chicken eggs instead of eggs that have been boiled. She has also used duck eggs. And she has one example of an ostrich egg she decorated with an intricate scene of The Last Supper.

The Staroschaks have a son, Myron, and a daughter, Zina. Myron's two daughters, Christina and Natalie, have taken up the pysanky tradition. The two teenage girls have demonstrated their knowledge to friends and neighbors in Houston where they lived for a time, thousands of miles from Ukraine where the art was perfected and hundreds of miles away from their grandparents' home in McKees Rocks where the art is still practiced with pride and meticulous attention to detail.

But distance is no barrier to the Staroschaks and the art of pysanky. Joanne and her husband have made two trips to Brazil, where she has demonstrated pysanky to Ukrainian communities there, and the couple also has traveled back to the Mother Country, where the art is treasured more now than ever before. Joanne has earned many honors for her work in passing on the Ukrainian legacy. She has appeared on television and has been interviewed for magazines and newspapers. She is a long-time participant in the Pittsburgh Folk Art Festival held in the late spring of each year, where she demonstrates her skill and creativity. One of her highest achievements came recently when the Ukrainian Technological Society of Pittsburgh awarded her its highest honor.

"I came to this country and the people here gave me the opportunity for a better life," Joanne observes. "I feel that it is my duty to give something back and that is what I try to do. Keeping traditions alive is a way of life for me and I can imagine no better life than one like this where a teacher can pass on what she knows and feels to others."

Above: *Learning from Mary Holtzman and William Johnson, Alexander Kipphut tries on a Scottish costume at Graeme Park's Scottish Heritage Festival.* **Above Right:** *Ewa and Buc Syski wear costumes from Poland to the Polish festival held annually at The National Shrine of Our Lady of Czestochowa near Doylestown. Ewa arrived from Krosniewice, Poland, within the past year.* **Right:** *Followers of Hinduism gather at the Hindu Association of Religion Institute (HARI) temple in York County to hear Shri Rameshbhai Oza, a guru from Mumbai, India.*

CHARLES L. BLOCKSON

While most children his age were thinking of school recess or pretty girls, Charles L. Blockson, was accumulating one of the nation's largest private collections of items related to black history and traditions. Forty years later, he is a recognized authority on African-American history and resources. Curator of a library bearing his name in the Special Collections Department of Temple University, Blockson has more than 150,000 books, manuscripts, broadsides, maps, and artifacts spanning nearly four centuries in areas of Africa, Europe, and the Caribbean, as well as the United States.

It is no accident that coverage of Pennsylvania's black heritage is prominent in the collection's treasures.

Born in Norristown, just outside of Philadelphia, in 1933, Blockson is author of numerous books and wrote the July 1984 National Geographic cover article on the Underground Railroad.

What spurred him to become a bibliophile and curator at a young age? Blockson recalls a moment when he was nine years old. "I was in school one morning and the teacher was speaking about Benjamin Franklin. As I listened to a litany of Franklin's accomplishments, it struck me that all the historic achievements that we had learned were credited to white Americans. I remembered discussions in my family, stories of Booker T. Washington, George Washington Carver, Joe Louis, Paul Robeson, and Jesse Owens."

Charles L. Blockson, curator of African-American documents and artifacts, in his Temple University office

There were three or four other black students in the class at the time, and Blockson asked the teacher if she could relate some notable contributions of black people. He wanted to know of other heroes he could look up to.

In his autobiography, *Damn Rare*, Blockson writes, "My teacher betrayed no hint of uncertainty. 'Negroes have no history. They were born to serve white people.' I sat stunned. For the first few moments after her retort, I was dreadfully aware of the sea of white faces surrounding us in the classroom. I had never before been confronted with such flagrant prejudice."

It was impossible, Blockson recalls, to deal with such brutal and demeaning attitudes at that time, but the teacher's response triggered a passion to dispel the myth she associated with his race. That passion follows him wherever he goes. Blockson became determined to excel on a personal level. At Norristown High School he starred in football and track and was offered scholarships by 60 colleges. He accepted an offer from Penn State, and became a track champion and, alternately with his roommate, Rosey Grier, set records in shot put and discus throw.

After graduating in 1956 and declining numerous offers to play professional football, Blockson spent two years in the U.S. Army and, upon his discharge, opened a janitorial service. In 1972 he joined the Norristown Area High School as an advisory specialist in human relations and cultural affairs. Working under the superintendent of schools, he spent time lecturing in the schools on African-American history, recruiting black faculty, and dealing with race related matters. All the while he pursued his passion for collecting, preserving, and promoting the study of African-American history.

As a teenager he was known among second-hand store proprietors and rare book dealers. Often, friends he made along the way would hold items for him, knowing the special place the artifact or book would have in his collection. One such occasion produced a copy of Harriet Beecher Stowe's A Key to *Uncle Tom's Cabin*, while another produced a find that stuns visitors as it must have stunned Blockson when he held it for the first time.

In a room of his archives at Temple, Blockson slides a glass door on a shelf and reaches for a volume covered in a black binding. He opens the book and points to the title, *Lincoln the Unknown*. The cover was made in 1933 from the skin of a black patient in a Baltimore hospital. Blockson believes that someone who hated both President Abraham Lincoln and blacks commissioned the special edition.

Blockson's achievements are well documented, but his drive seems unlimited. Founder of the Afro-American Historical and Cultural Museum in Philadelphia, he has also served as president of the Pennsylvania Abolition Society. He was a member of the State Historical and Record Advisory Board for Pennsylvania and its Black History Advisory Board. The United States Secretary of the Interior appointed him as chair of the Underground Railroad Advisory Committee and, from 1990 to 1995, he directed the National Park Services' publications, including *The Underground Railroad* (Handbook # 156) and *The Official Map and Guide to the Underground Railroad*.

His travels take him from Paris to the Caribbean and from Senegal to Zaire, when he is not tracing routes of the Underground Railroad in Pennsylvania and nearby states. "The Caribbean islands were a stopping-off place for Africans en route to lives of servitude," he reminds visitors. "They were used as a place where Africans could be 'seasoned,' before they were transported to the slave markets.

"We must include these islands when we study the history of African-Americans. Surprising to many contemporary students, slaves were held in Pennsylvania.

"We need to commemorate sites connected to black history, not commercialize them," he says with a fiery passion. This passion he feels was translated in 1989 into a project commemorating the contributions of African-Americans to Philadelphia and the world.

In a special project supported by the Pennsylvania Historical and Museum Commission and other agencies, 65 historical markers have been erected. That project resulted in another Blockson publication, *Philadelphia's Guide: African-American State Historical Markers*.

Recounting the lasting contributions of blacks to Pennsylvania and the nation, Blockson notes, "They are all around us." He cites the fashion of braiding hair and summarizes the effect on musical taste, from gospel to jazz, blues to rap. "The contributions are everywhere," he says. "Billboards and television ads feature beautiful black models. Look at the menus in restaurants, where soul food is not the only term with an African past. Men and women from many backgrounds are adopting the practice of body piercing that has been popular in Africa since ancient times.

"Consider the use of phrases in modern English like 'Oh, Man!' and 'Go, Girl.' These are examples of African influence that grow with time"

Blockson believes that in many ways African-Americans have lost their sense of community, but he also sees a revived interest in the history of black people.

"No race of people should be deprived of the knowledge of itself," he concludes, "and to understand where we are going, we must know where we have been."

Left: *Abrianne Rhoad, 4th grader at Herbert Hoover Elementary School, Linglestown, lights the seventh candle on the sixth day of Kwanzaa, which honors creativity,* kuumba *in Swahili.* **Top:** *Making quilts for fundraisers fuels the tradition of quilt making. This annual quilt auction at the Central Pennsylvania Relief Sale brings in thousands of dollars to benefit the service projects of the Mennonite Central Committee worldwide.* **Above:** *A Harrisburg family celebrates Hannukah, a Jewish holiday season of candles and gifts.*

Ethnic costumes often denote particular geographic regions or clan affiliation and frequently display local artistry in the stitchery. Machine embroidery and hand needlework such as counted cross-stitch and crocheted lace decorate ethnic garb. Costumes add a dramatic dimension to folk dancing and other celebratory occasions. These costume details, often on the front bodice, were photographed at an ethnic costume exhibit at the Pittsburgh Folk Festival.

Sporran (pouch) worn in front of Scottish Highlander's kilt

Greek

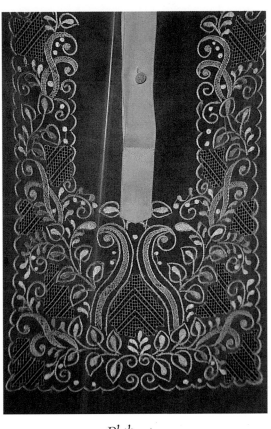

Philippine

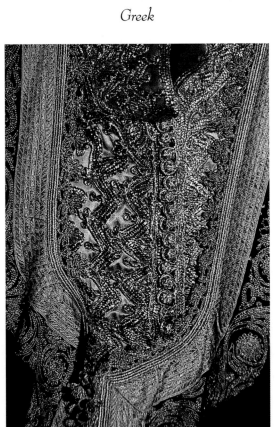

Indian

Hungarian

Ukrainian

Chinese

Greek

Scandinavian

152

Lithuanian

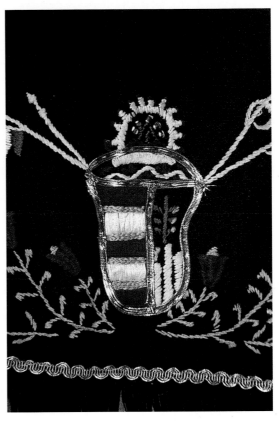

Hungarian

Slovakian

Serbian

153

Previous Pages: *Carving a roasted turkey at the Christmas table is a family tradition practiced by many ethnic groups.* **Top:** *A Ukrainian doll and wheat sheaf complement a Christmas tree.* **Above Left:** *Handmade Serbian ornaments decorate a tree.* **Above Right:** *At Bethlehem, this tree decorated in the Irish tradition is displayed with other national trees.* **Right:** *Swedish-American families attend the Lucia Fest each December at the American Swedish Historical Museum in Philadelphia. Wearing a crown of lighted candles, Tiffany Gould as Lucia leads a procession of girls in white with tinsel in their hair.*

SELECTED BIBLIOGRAPHY

_____. *The Italians in Pennsylvania*, Pamphlet No. 4. The Pennsylvania Historical and Museum Commission, Harrisburg, Pennsylvania, 1998.

Applebome, Peter. *Dixie Rising*. Harcourt, Brace & Co., New York, New York, 1996.

Bazelon, Bruce. *The Jews in Pennsylvania*, Pamphlet No. 2. The Pennsylvania Historical and Museum Commission, Harrisburg, Pennsylvania, 1986.

Beyer, George R., ed. *Guide to the State Historical Markers of Pennsylvania*. The Pennsylvania Historical and Museum Commission, Harrisburg, Pennsylvania, 1991.

Blockson, Charles L. *Damn Rare: The Memoirs of An African-American Bibliophile*. Quantum Leap Publisher, Tracy, California, 1998.

Bronner, Simon J. *Popularizing Pennsylvania: Henry W. Shoemaker and the Progressive Uses of Folklore and History*. The Pennsylvania State University, University Park, Pennsylvania, 1996.

Casey, Betty. *International Folk Dance*. Doubleday & Co., Inc., Garden City, New York, 1981.

Cowan, Paul. *The Tribes of America: Journalistic Discoveries of Our People and Their Cultures*. Doubleday & Co., Garden City, New York, 1979.

Earnest, Russell D., and Corinne P. *Papers for Birth Dayes: Guide to the Fraktur Artists and Scriveners, Vol. 1, 2nd edition*. Russell E. Earnest Associates, East Berlin, Pennsylvania, 1997.

Ebert, Catherine and John, eds. *American Folk Art Painters*. Scribners, New York, New York, 1975.

Fortenbaugh, Robert T., and Tarman, H. James. *Pennsylvania: The Story of a Commonwealth*. Pennsylvania Book Service, Harrisburg, Pennsylvania, 1940.

Gregory, Richard L., ed. *The Oxford Companion to the Mind*. Oxford University Press, Oxford, England, and New York, New York, 1987.

Groff, Betty. *Betty Groff's Pennsylvania Dutch Cookbook*. Macmillan Publishing Company, New York, New York, 1990.

Hopkins, Leroy, and Smith, Eric Ledell. *The African Americans in Pennsylvania*, Pamphlet No. 6. The Pennsylvania Historical and Museum Commission, Harrisburg, Pennsylvania, 1984.

Hubbert-Kemper, Ruthann, Clymer, Paul I., *et al. Preserving a Palace of Art, A Guide to the Projects of the Pennsylvania Capitol Preservation Committee*. Pennsylvania Capitol Preservation Committee, Harrisburg, Pennsylvania, 2000.

Hulan, Richard H. *The Swedes in Pennsylvania*, Pamphlet No. 5. The Pennsylvania Historical and Museum Commission, Harrisburg, Pennsylvania, 1994.

Kent, Barry C. *Susquehanna's Indians*. Commonwealth of Pennsylvania and The Pennsylvania Historical and Museum Commission, Harrisburg, Pennsylvania, 1984.

Klees, Fredric. *The Pennsylvania Dutch*. The Macmillan Company, New York, New York, 1961.

Magda, Matthew S. *The Welsh in Pennsylvania*, Pamphlet No. 1. The Pennsylvania Historical and Museum Commission, Harrisburg, Pennsylvania, 1998.

Magda, Matthew S. *The Poles in Pennsylvania*, Pamphlet No. 3. The Pennsylvania Historical and Museum Commission, Harrisburg, Pennsylvania, 1986.

Martin, Jere. *Pennsylvania Almanac*. Stackpole Books, Mechanicsburg, Pennsylvania, 1997.

Nagurny, Kyle. *The Pennsylvania Heritage Cookbook: A Cook's Tour of Keystone Cultures, Customs and Celebrations*. Stackpole Books, Mechanicsburg, Pennsylvania, 1998.

Newhouse, Elizabeth L., *et al*, eds. *America's Historic Places*., National Geographic Society, Washington, D. C., 1996.

Seitz, Ruth Hoover, and Seitz, Blair. *Philadelphia*. RB Books, Harrisburg, Pennsylvania, 1994.

Seitz, Ruth Hoover, and Seitz, Blair. *Pittsburgh*. RB Books, Harrisburg, Pennsylvania, 1997.

Sheedy, Madelon U., ed. *Jacob Eicholtz (1776-1842)*. Southern Alleghenies Museum of Art at Ligonier Valley, Ligonier, Pennsylvania, 1997.

Staub, Shalom D., ed. *Craft and Community: Traditional Arts in Contemporary Society*. Catalogue for An Exhibition Organized by the Museum of the Balch Institute for Ethnic Studies and the Pennsylvania Heritage Affairs Commission, The Balch Institute and the Pennsylvania Heritage Affairs Commission, Philadelphia, Pennsylvania, 1988.

Thernstrom, Stephan, ed. *The Harvard Encyclopedia of American Ethnic Groups*. Harvard University Press, Cambridge, Massachusetts, 1981.

Upton, Dell, ed. *America's Architectural Roots: Ethnic Groups That Built America*. The Preservation Press, National Trust for Historic Preservation, Washington, D.C., 1986.

Weiser, Frederick S., *et al*, eds. *Der Reggeboge (The Rainbow)*. Pamphlet Newsletter, Quarterly of the Pennsylvania German Society, Brenigsville, Pennsylvania, all issues, University of Pennsylvania, Philadelphia, Pennsylvania.

Whiffen, Marcus, and Koeper, Frederick. *American Architecture, Vols. 1 and II*. The MIT Press, Cambridge, Massachusetts, 1981.

Wolf, Edwin, 2nd. *Philadelphia, Portrait of An American City*. The William Penn Foundation, Stackpole Books, Harrisburg, Pennsylvania, 1975.

Yoder, Don, *et al. Pennsylvania Folklife*, Member Magazine, Pennsylvania Folklife Society, Lancaster, Pennsylvania, all issues, University of Pennsylvania, Philadelphia, Pennsylvania.

INDEX

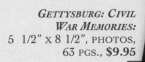

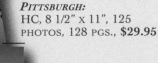

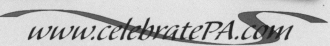